CRITICAL THINKING

AN INTRODUCTION TO

CRITICAL THINKING

Madhucchanda Sen

Pearson

ISBN 978-81-317-3456-8

First Impression 2010
Eleventh Impression 2022
Twelth Impression 2024

Published by Pearson India Education Services Pvt. Ltd, CIN: U72200TN2005PTC057128

Head Office: 1st Floor, Berger Tower, Plot No. C-001A/2, Sector 16B, Noida – 201 301,Uttar Pradesh, India.

Registered Office: Featherlite, 'The Address' 5th Floor, Survey No 203/10B, 200 Ft MMRD Road,Zamin Pallavaram, Chennai - 600044
Website: in.pearson.com; Email:companysecretary.india@pearson.com

Digitally printed in India by Trinity Academy for Corporate Training Ltd, New Delhi in the year of 2024.

In the loving memory of
my father
Professor Pranab Kumar Sen
and for
my mother
Mrs Rama Sen
who encouraged me to think for myself

CONTENTS

PREFACE AND ACKNOWLEDGEMENTS

Human beings develop at two levels. First, they develop as individuals, and then they develop as members of a society. They can be said to have developed as individuals when they begin to *think for themselves*. Similarly, they can be said to have developed into mature social individuals when they become capable of understanding and evaluating the world around them, and are able to take decisions independently and responsibly. Along our journey of becoming rational, social, and moral agents, one thing that comes most handy is critical thinking. Critical thinking is an area of study which has now been recognised as being relevant to students and scholars in all domains. The reason is that the ability to think clearly and rationally is important for everyone, no matter what she chooses to do in life. This is why we cannot restrict critical thinking skills to any specific area. It is relevant for those in education, especially research, and is equally relevant for people working in the field of finance, management, legal profession and also for people in politics. In a globalised world, the phenomenon of information explosion requires one to be intellectually flexible. Critical thinking skills bring in this flexibility. It also brings in the desired creativity of the mind that helps one to come up with new solutions to age-old problems. Above all, an unreflective life is not worth living. Anyone who engages in self-reflection is already a critical thinker. This book is just an introduction to this very fascinating area of study. The purpose of this book will be served if young thinkers find it relevant and realise the importance, the joys and the responsibilities of thinking for oneself.

Many people have assisted me in writing this book. I would like to first mention Debjani Dutta and Arani Banerjee of Pearson Education for asking me to write the book in the first place; special thanks to Preeta Priyamvada for her excellent editorial assistance. I must express my gratitude to my mother who has assisted me in every possible way so that I could meet the deadlines, and my sons Aban and Arka who have quite sportingly accepted the sheer neglect that I inflicted upon them for completing this book! Last but not the least, I must thank my husband Nirmalya for his encouragement and for providing research material for my work.

Madhucchanda Sen

1

WHAT IS CRITICAL THINKING?

Socrates: ... the unexamined life is not worth living.

—Plato, Apology[1]

1.1 Introduction

When I started studying philosophy as an undergraduate student, a teacher of mine told us in his very first lecture, "If you want to be a good philosopher, you need to give up two senses—the sense of obviousness and the sense of absurdity". Critical thinking makes you a good philosopher in this way. By a philosopher, we do not mean a practising philosopher but what may be called a wise person, a person adept with skills that will help her to smoothly steer her way through the complexities that this world and life present. Philosophy makes a person an intellectually responsible adult, one who is able to think through things in ways that enable one to evaluate one's circumstances and take intelligent decisions. These decisions could be of many kinds—a decision about whom to marry, which route to take to reach one's destination while driving, deciding which of the many competing scientific theories that claim to solve a question of science is more acceptable, deciding which political party to vote for, how to solve a stalemate between one's colleagues or even finding a credible way of convincing a friend not to take up drugs. In each case, what is required is a kind of intellectual integrity. Critical thinking helps us in achieving this intellectual integrity. Let us see how this takes place.

1.2 Who Is a Critical Thinker?

Any student who asks the general question, "Why should we think critically?" or the more specific question, "Why am I required to do a course on critical thinking?" is a critical thinker already. Whenever we ask for the reasons behind something, we are thinking critically. Doing so does not require us to be particularly intelligent or gifted, nor does it require us to be logicians or argumentative lawyers. Whenever we question the methods of persuasion that are thrust upon us to make us believe or do things, we are thinking critically. Why should I not smoke? Why should I vote for Party A instead of Party B? Why should I buy a shampoo with pro-vitamins? Why should I invest in this mutual fund rather than that? Why should I think that globalisation is bad? Why should I support Greenpeace? Why should I not eat junk food? Why should I take job A instead of job B? Why should I believe that our economy is sound? Why is cloning bad? Why is abortion unethical? Why should I believe in God? Why should I take your word against my friend's? Why should I believe whatever my elders say?

All these questions reflect that the person who is asking these questions is asking for justifications for either doing or not doing something and for believing or not believing something. Being sceptical is a virtue of the critical mind. Young people, by nature, have questioning minds. But one does not become a critical thinker by merely questioning everything with a vengeance. Being reasonable is also a virtue of a mature critical mind. We must remember that in being a critical thinker, what we reflect is not only some intellectual skill (like the skill that is required for being good at chess or Sudoku), but we must also reflect a sense of intellectual responsibility, which any adult human being ought to have. Thought, after all, is a human action. Like all other human actions, we may be held responsible for our thoughts too, and they are also open to evaluation. Hence, we may be worthy of praise if we think in ways that reflect intellectual responsibility, and worthy of blame if we are callous or wrong. We have to remember that as adults we need to think things through for ourselves and also think them through well. We cannot, as responsible adults, shrug off our responsibilities in thought just as much as we cannot do so in action.

1.2.1 Who Is a Good Critical Thinker and Who Isn't?

If we reflect a little, we shall see that people who answer these questions in the best possible ways are able to convince and persuade us. We would quickly realise that there are ways of persuasion that are good or effective, and there are other ways that are simply bad or ineffective.

KEY POINTS

Who is a critical thinker?

- ❑ A person who asks for justifications or reasons
- ❑ A person who is sceptical
- ❑ A person who is intellectually responsible

THINKING THROUGH EXERCISE 1

(i) What is the necessity to become a critical thinker?

(ii) Which of the following terms and phrases are most closely related to critical thinking and why?

- ❑ Intelligence
- ❑ Common sense
- ❑ Reasonableness
- ❑ Imagination
- ❑ Social responsibility
- ❑ Intellectual responsibility

If your parents told you not to smoke and you asked, "Why not?" and they replied, "Because *we* told you not to," it is more likely that you would continue smoking. But if, instead, they told you that smoking causes cancer, you would think twice before smoking.

A person who is good at persuasion is a good critical thinker. A person who is good at deciding whether a mode of persuasion is good or not is also a good critical thinker. In each case, we realise how important it is to be a good critical thinker. Not only do we need to convince others about things we believe but we also need to figure out in a particular situation whether we should be convinced about something. But how do we gear up to become good critical thinkers?

Suppose you have a problem with your knee. Would you go to your childhood paediatrician because you are so emotionally attached to her that you cannot think of going to any other doctor? If you did, you would be considered downright irrational. In making a rational or wise decision about things like this, we need to exercise *reason* and should not be guided by *emotion*. Instead, consider a scenario in which you decide to seek the best orthopaedist in town to solve your problem with your knee and you find out that Dr B is the best and has successfully operated on your friend's knee. In this scenario, suppose you choose to ignore the fact that he was not so successful when he treated another friend's mother's arthritis, in all probabilities you would end up disappointed with Dr B. In this case, you started off well because you realised that you needed *reasons* or *evidence* to back your belief in Dr B. But you still failed at your attempt at thinking critically because you did not really consider *all* the evidence. Being rational therefore does not always mean being right. Being rational involves the ability to judge what would be the best course of action and what would be the best explanation in any circumstance.

1.2.2 Marks of a Fair Critical Thinker

We often hear about neutral umpires in cricket matches. Cricket selectors choose umpires who do not have any relation with the contenders of the match because their decisions are regarded as *free of motive and bias*. A motivated or biased judgement is always to be avoided. In order to ensure our own judgements are objective, we need to be *self-aware*, that is, capable of understanding our own *assumptions, prejudices, perspectives* and *biases*. When we are able to do so, we become *fair critical thinkers*—thinkers who are not swayed by selfish motives, emotional impulses or even self-deception.

Fairness arises from *open-mindedness*. A fair judge is also an open-minded person. In evaluating a case, one must be able to consider all the possible and reasonable inferences as well as all the possible points of view. The ability to realise that there may be different interpretations of the same case is the clear mark of a critical thinker. The ability to accept new explanations, new theories, new paradigms and models is also the mark of a good theoretician in general and a good scientist in particular, both of whom are examples of critical thinkers.

Achieving all this is not an easy task. A person may be well trained in logic and yet might find it difficult to be fair, unbiased and actually might fail to exercise her critical skills to the fullest. In fact, most of the crises the world is facing today are due to narrow, lop-sided or simplistic views of the world that most of us have. Political stalemates result when people see things in black and white and fail to see the nuances and subtleties of the issues at hand. Crises emerge when leaders fail to see the different strands that make up a complex situation, when people are unable to have a holistic understanding of events. A certain amount of self-discipline is required to become a critical thinker and, in turn, responsible citizens of the world. For this, we must have a good understanding of the standards of critical thinking.

KEY POINTS

Who is a good critical thinker?

- ❑ One who is guided by reason
- ❑ One who is not guided just by emotions
- ❑ One who considers all the evidence at hand and follows the route that the evidence points towards
- ❑ One who is in search for the best explanation
- ❑ One who is free from motives or biases
- ❑ One who is aware of her own prejudices
- ❑ One who is fair and open minded

THINKING THROUGH EXERCISE 2

(i) What are the self-directed and other-directed aspects of critical thinking?

(ii) What could make us jump to the wrong conclusions or lead us to make wrong judgements?

(iii) Who is a fair critical thinker?

(iv) Why do we need to be open-minded in critical thinking?

1.3 Standards of Critical Thinking

Standards of critical thinking are those criteria in the light of which we may evaluate whether one's thinking or reasoning process is critical or good. These are benchmarks that help us to write, think and evaluate issues in a way that reflects our *intellectual responsibility*. We shall discuss the important criteria of critical thinking, although it is entirely possible to come up with more criteria than those we cover here.

1.3.1 Clarity

In thinking critically, the first and foremost standard that we need to achieve is *clarity*. Being able to *speak and write clearly* is essential to any exercise that involves critical thought. If I am not able to clearly state my case, no one can evaluate what I say as either true or relevant or worth listening to. Being clear is also essential for *effective communication*.

Let us take a common real-life situation. Suppose you want to buy a ticket to go to Agra from New Delhi and you say to the man at the ticket counter, "Ticket from New Delhi to Agra". The vagueness of this request would exasperate the teller who would rightfully ask you to fill in a requisition slip available at the booking counter. This slip helps you to be clear and specific with your request by asking about details such as which train you want to travel by; which date you want to travel on; which station you would embark from; where you want to disembark; how many individuals would be travelling; their names, age and sex; whether there would be any children travelling etc. This example shows the necessity of being clear in speech and thought in order to be understood first and then evaluated.

When someone is *vague, imprecise, obscure* or *confused*, it is difficult to gauge what she is saying. Vagueness also depends on one's audience. When a doctor tells a lay patient in medical terms what their problem is, she might find it very obscure, although it may make perfect sense to another doctor. The doctor might then express it in common language so that the patient understands the problem clearly.

This is exactly the kind of process science teachers undertake when teaching very young children about basic scientific concepts. For instance, suppose you need to explain to a child what a neuron is. You might say that they are small messengers that carry news from one part of the body to another, and this might help the child understand. Of course, one would not use the same kind of explanation with all audiences. Notice, for instance, how political leaders' speech changes with the audience that they are addressing. The words that they use when addressing daily wage earners will not be the words they use when addressing businessmen. The examples that they use to illustrate their points also change with the context and audience. This shows how *clarity is context sensitive*.

Sometimes we use certain *concepts* without having a clear idea about them. For example, the concept of secularism, which we so often use in the Indian context, is a concept about which most Indians have no clear idea. It is only when we are asked, "But what do you mean by 'secular'?" that we stop and try to analyse what exactly it means. *Conceptual clarity* is essential to a critical thinker.

One profession that requires a high degree of conceptual clarity is teaching. Experts on critical thinking say, "Your thinking is clear when you can state your meaning exactly, when you can elaborate on it and explain it, when you can give good examples and illustrations of it".[2] Good teachers, orators and speakers all try to do this. One needs to be clear in two ways. First, one needs to be clear about what one means, believes or thinks. Second, one has to find a clear way of expressing what is on one's mind so that the audience is able to grasp the intended meaning. Therefore, clarity should be exercised both for oneself and for others. These two are related because a person needs to be clear in her mind in order to be able to express her thoughts clearly to others. Let us see how we can be clear in our own minds and how we may express what is on our minds clearly to others.

In our own case

- We should be able to *clearly articulate* what we precisely mean.
- If asked, we should be able to *elaborate* any point that we make.
- We should be able to come up with as many *illustrations* as required to express our point.
- We should *re-evaluate* the words and modes of explanation we use to clarify things further in our mind.
- We should think about *the audience* we are addressing and accordingly envisage difficulties that they might have in understanding what we say.
- We should be able to *analyse* any concept that we use.
- We should be able to *rephrase* whatever we say.
- We should be able to judge hypothetical cases.

In the case of others

- We should say only that which we ourselves understand clearly.
- We should at all times encourage questions from our audience and try to answer them.
- We should ask our audience from time to time what they understood from our own exposition—this is a clear indication of whether we have succeeded in communicating our intended message.
- We should ask our audience to reflect on the issue in their own way and be open to new ways of looking at any issue.

There are many problems or *impediments to being clear*. One of the greatest impediments is lack of clarity of thought, which is often the cause of the lack of clarity in articulation. We often believe things in a rather *unreflecting* way. We then find it hard to make our meaning clear to others when asked for clarifications simply because we have not quite thought it through in our own minds. The lack of sense of *intellectual responsibility* and a *casual approach* to issues are often responsible for this sort of unclearness of the mind.

There are several other impediments to clarity of thought. One such impediment is *prejudice* that clouds our thoughts, making them vague and obscure. Very often, we are unable to think or talk clearly if we are overcome by some *strong emotions* such as fear, anger or even depression. Another reason we are often unclear is that we do not understand that what seems clear or obvious to us may be confusing and unclear for our audience.

THINKING THROUGH EXERCISE 3

(i) Why do we need to think and speak clearly?

(ii) Why is clarity context-sensitive? Explain with the help of an example.

(iii) Take a concept we often use and test if we are clear about it. Try to clarify it. (Suggested examples: *Success*, *Development*, *Intelligence*, *Secularism*, *A Fast Bowler*, *Smart*, *Profit*, *Equality*)

(iv) Explain what clarity means in one's own case and what it means in the case of others.

(v) What are the barriers to clarity?

1.3.2 Accuracy

Being accurate means being *true to the facts*. As a child, I heard a story about an emperor and his servant. The servant once asked why the emperor paid such a fat salary to his prime minister and not to the servant who worked hard all day long. In reply, the emperor asked the servant to go inside the palace and find out about the queen's pet cat who was supposed to be delivering her litter at any time. The servant rushed back with the news that the cat had just had her litter. The emperor asked the servant, "How many?" The servant did not know, so he rushed back inside the palace and came back with the answer: four. The emperor asked how many of the kittens were male and how many female. The servant could not answer. He again rushed into the palace and came back with the answer: three males and one female. The emperor then asked whether the mother cat and her babies were all in good health and again the poor servant had to run inside the palace to find out the answer. Having finished with the servant, the emperor then called his prime minister and told him that the queen's cat had just had her litter. He asked the prime minister to go inside the palace and bring him news of the cat and her babies. The prime minister on his return said to the emperor: "The cat has had four babies, of which three are male and one female. The cat and the babies are all in good health." This simple story speaks volumes of the importance of accuracy.

We know how important accuracy is when making quantitative judgements in science. In a scientific experiment, we know we cannot give merely rough estimates of, for instance, the weight of a chemical substance, as we may do when describing the weight of some food item we purchased from the market. However, when buying the food item, we demand an accurate estimate of its weight from the seller whom we are paying for it and are very cautious about whether the seller's weighing scale is accurate.

We also understand the importance of accuracy when we are exasperated and infuriated by inaccurate news reports in newspapers or on television. Newspaper publishing houses and news channels can even be legally punished if their reports are found to be inaccurate.

It is important to point out a key difference here—*clarity and accuracy are not the same.* I may be clear without being accurate. For instance, "Dogs generally live up to the age of fifteen" is a clear statement but an inaccurate one. *A statement is accurate if it is true, confirmed by evidence, defended by justifications, corroborated by facts, authenticated by testimony and is guaranteed and established.* One must remember that sometimes a question of truth is replaced by a question of accuracy. There are certain statements that can be declared as outright true or false whereas with others we cannot make straightforward claims of the truth. In such cases, we speak of accuracy i.e., of evidential support, justification, etc.

In our day-to-day lives, we make many kinds of statements. Some of them are strictly factual and can be easily judged as true or false and hence accurate or inaccurate. For example, the statement, "London is the capital of UK," is a simple fact. There can be other kinds of statements that are not factual but can be proved to be true by the exercise of reason, for example, "7 + 5 = 12". There is still more kinds of statements that are neither accurate nor inaccurate. For instance, with statements like, "Globalisation is destroying regional cultures," it is difficult to reach a consensus regarding their truth, but we may look for accuracy on the basis of the kind of evidence that does not entail the truth.

Just as in the case of clarity, we can also take several measures to be accurate in our thinking and while speaking to others.

In our own case

- ❑ We should be critical before accepting any information as true or accurate and must *judge the credibility of the source* of each piece of information.
- ❑ We must *review all our beliefs* with the eye of a sceptic. We must not accept them as the truth right from the beginning but think of them as working hypotheses, leaving room for doubt and awaiting confirmation.
- ❑ We often believe what we wish to be true. We must be careful about this tendency.
- ❑ We must examine the accuracy of what we believe, of what we read, of what we hear and also of what is usually accepted as truth by the majority. In doing this, we have to continuously question the source of information, judge the reliability of the source, not accept anything that seems to be true or right without scrutiny, apply suitable methods of scrutinising "facts", and always try to think of counter examples.

In the case of others

- ❑ We should be open to the doubts of the audience.
- ❑ We should ask our audience to point out which parts of our exposition they think are inaccurate or doubtful.
- ❑ We should find out which of our statements appeared to be unsupported to the audience and try our level best to support them.

There are many *impediments to thinking accurately.* Sometimes it is difficult to scrutinise our resources because there are not that many resources available and therefore *not many resources to compare and judge for accuracy.* There are areas of knowledge for which we have to depend on just a single expert or resource. When there is just one resource, however, it is hard to judge if it is accurate as there is no alternative to compare it with.

THINKING THROUGH EXERCISE 4

(i) What is the relation between truth and accuracy?
(ii) What is clarity for oneself and what is clarity with respect to others?
(iii) What are the barriers to clarity?

Sometimes we become so *comfortable with our long-held beliefs* that we experience a kind of inertia in questioning them. This often leads us to believe what we wish to be true and blinds us to the alternatives.

Sometimes, we just make *hasty generalisations* and can be led astray by *emotional experiences.* For instance, a person who has had a traumatic experience in a particular foreign country at once becomes xenophobic about that country and makes hasty generalisations about it. This in turn leads to inaccurate judgements about its people.

Often, we are unable to see the flaws in our own arguments, though we are able to pick out flaws in the arguments of others. This is why all honest writers want others to proofread their work as they realise that their own flaws would not be visible to their own eyes.

We also often tend to hold beliefs that have turned into platitudes or clichés that have been culturally or socially held by vast majorities for many years. In the face of counter evidence, we find it hard to let go of such long-held beliefs and accept new truths in spite of sufficient evidence supporting them. We feel *comfortable with our old folk beliefs* and find it hard to judge their accuracy and truth.

In modern times, the media has taken the place of folk beliefs. So good has it been at doing this that we now find it very hard to doubt what we see in print. The media seems to exercise a kind of authority over us, which makes us extremely *gullible.* This situation worsens when the media caters to our wishes by giving us the kind of news that our heart desires to hear as opposed to the kind of news that our heads would judge as accurate.

All this makes being an accurate thinker extremely difficult. Therefore, one has to be on a constant vigil to guard against all kinds of *inaccuracies and biases.*

1.3.3 Precision

Precision is a standard of critical thinking that is closely tied with accuracy, as one cannot be precise without being accurate. *One can however be accurate without being precise.* For instance, I might say that it gets very hot during May in Kolkata, and this would be fairly accurate. To be precise, however, I would have to provide statistics of the temperatures of Kolkata during the month of May for the last ten years. In this way, my accurate statement also becomes precise. *In being precise, we become more specific and do not omit any details that are relevant to substantiate a claim.*

When you want to convince people about what you think, you cannot just make vague and general remarks; you must be specific enough to convey the exact point you wish to drive home. Clarity, accuracy and precision all go together and this is best illustrated in the story of the emperor and his servant in the previous section. In this story, the servant's report of the cat's litter was accurate, but the prime minister's report was clear, accurate and, most importantly, precise, giving his audience all the details that were required and hence not leaving much room for further questions or doubts.

The need for precision is felt in every day life. When a doctor asks his patient to keep a temperature chart rather than just saying that she has had a fever for the last four days, the doctor is demanding precision to help him make a diagnosis and decide the course of his treatment.

The need for precision and the need for a particular degree of precision are both *relative to the context* at hand. For instance, when we say we want a hundred grams of butter, it does not much concern us if the quantity we are given is more or less by half a gram. It is a situation in which precision is not of great importance. But when in a chemistry laboratory conducting an experiment, we will try to be as precise as possible in our measurements.

In certain spheres, the details are less important than the overall picture. In such a case, precision is a lesser virtue than a holistic appraisal of the situation at hand. Often, we might get bogged down by the little details and miss the *holistic picture* that emerges from putting all of these details in the right perspective. For instance, we may have detailed statistics on voting patterns among working women over the past fifteen years in Kerala, but unless we analyse this data and make significant political or socio-economic inferences about the relation between voting patterns, women employment and women empowerment, this statistical data would be of little significance to social sciences.

In the case of precision too, we may take measures to be precise with respect to our own thinking and also with respect to how precisely we are able to communicate our thoughts to others.

In our own case

- ❑ We should be able to see if our own statements are *substantiated by details* or not. If we find that they lack specific details, we must find ways to gather those details.
- ❑ We should try to *provide* as much *detailed information* as possible on a particular issue.
- ❑ We should gather detailed information from resourceful people, from texts, from any *credible source* that we can avail of. But in doing so we must exercise cautious scrutiny.
- ❑ We should be equally comfortable with *moving from the general to specifics as* we are with moving from specifics to the general.

In the case of others

- ❑ We should be *open to suggestions* from our audience regarding the lack of details in our statements.
- ❑ We should take the help of fellow enquirers and our audiences in locating gaps in our argument where we need a more detailed exposition.

THINKING THROUGH EXERCISE 5

(i) Why do we need to be precise?
(ii) Why is precision context sensitive?
(iii) What is precision for oneself and what is it in the case of others?
(iv) What are the barriers to precise thinking?

There are many an *impediment to thinking and speaking precisely.* One of these is that people are often unaware and *untrained* on speaking and thinking precisely. Often, the case at hand is so complicated that it needs special skills to gather the desired details to make our exposition precise. Probably the most serious difficulty in thinking and speaking precisely is that the *holistic picture often blurs out all the details* in a way that specificity and precision become rare to come by.

1.3.4 Relevance

A person who thinks about things that are irrelevant to the issue under enquiry or speaks about such irrelevant things cannot go far in the business of thinking critically. *While thinking through a problem, we must find out what is relevant or important for that problem.* We must find and enquire into all and only those things that are relevant to the problem.

For instance, suppose we are investigating the causes of global warming. In doing so, we must look into all the environmental changes and their causes that lead to global warming. There may also be some economic issues that are relevant to this problem. But if we think that the validity of some very technical micro-economic formula is equally relevant to it, we may be wrong. We may be equally wrong in thinking that issues relating to intellectual property rights or to fashion trends in the 1980s or 1990s are relevant to the problem of global warming.

We must have an eye for detecting what is relevant and what isn't. This is extremely important when, for instance, trying to make a breakthrough in the detection of the causes of a disease. There may be a large number of possible phenomena that we notice, but we have to be able to trace among them the relevant ones and make the required etiological breakthrough.

In deciding what is relevant for a particular question at hand, we have to remember that there may be many issues that are personally important to us, but they are not necessarily important for the problem in question. We should then be able to *set aside what is important for* us and concentrate only on issues that are directly or indirectly related to the question at hand.

Let's consider another example. Suppose your ancestors were displaced from their homeland and you have inherited strong feelings about their experience. When examining the issue of the refugee problem in other countries, Eastern European countries for instance, you may allow your investigation to be affected by your personal feelings, but that would be absolutely irrelevant to the issue at hand. This is because the socio-political situation of Eastern Europe is absolutely different from the one that resulted in your ancestors' migration.

We will now look into what measures we can take to find what is relevant to the problem in question with respect to our own thinking and also with respect to how relevantly we may handle the question while discussing it with others.

In our own case

- In order to find out which are the relevant issues to the problem at hand, we need to be thorough about the problem and in considering each possible related issue we need to ask the question, *"How is this connected with my main problem?"*
- At no point of the enquiry should we *lose sight of the main problem* under scrutiny.
- In order to achieve all this, we must always *review our course of thinking.*
- We should chalk out all the important points and sub-points.
- We should also make summaries and outlines.
- We should try to understand the relationships between the various concepts involved in the enquiry. For this, we can use "concept maps".
- We must *sift for the relevant issues* among all the peripheral ones, even if the peripheral issues are more interesting to us.

In the case of others

- We must seriously consider *what the audience considers relevant* to the enquiry.
- We must clearly indicate what we consider as important and also clarify what the audience considers important by asking questions, summarising and analysing.

Teachers often find it very difficult to mark the answer scripts of students who have filled page after page with information on a subject they have not been asked to write on. Students on their end find it hard to accept low marks on answers that they have laboriously written with a lot of details, simply because the teacher judges it as irrelevant. One of the greatest impediments to thinking in relevant ways is that we often feel that the more we say or the more we write, the better we have handled the problem. This, however, is a misconception. In our concern about the sheer volume of material we produce, we often lose sight of the main problem. In other words, we forget the larger and more critical issue in the course of being too meticulous and detailed. It is important to decide which details are relevant and not give all details an equal amount of importance indiscriminately. This is something we typically do when we are not spending time on proper reflection but just stating whatever comes to mind first.

In such cases, we may not realise that sometimes our emotional attachment with one aspect of a problem can cause us to ignore its other pressing aspects that in fact need more of our attention. We are often unable to put a finger on what is relevant because we consider a problem in isolation, whereas it should always be put in its actual context.

THINKING THROUGH EXERCISE 6

(i) Why do we need to find out what is relevant for our enquiry while thinking critically?

(ii) Can you think of a problem and then list its relevant and irrelevant factors? (Suggested example: You have a leaking pipe in your kitchen. You want to solve this problem. What are the factors that are relevant for you in doing so?)

(iii) How can we achieve relevance in our own case and how can we achieve it in the case of others?

(iv) What are the barriers to finding out what is relevant for an enquiry?

In spite of all the impediments to finding out and sticking to what is relevant, we often manage to succeed at doing this as can be seen in many people's ability to make lists of important or relevant things when solving problems so as to make their task easier to accomplish.

1.3.5 Depth

So far, we have seen that for thinking critically we need to be clear, accurate, and precise, and focus on what is relevant. Doing all this gives a certain amount of depth in handling a problem at hand. We realise that when we think critically, we get to the heart of a problem and undertake a *threadbare analysis* of it. Any sort of *half-hearted, superficial approach* is sure to have disastrous results.

If we want to achieve a certain amount of depth in our approach to a problem, we need to *look beyond the surface* and *get to the heart of the matter*. For example, usually we consider famines and floods as natural calamities. But we have now come to see through the eyes of various economists and sociologists how some famines and floods that may appear to be natural calamities are actually man made. This should help us realise that each problem has its own variety of complexities and only a critical mind is able to meander through them to come up with a *comprehensive analysis* and thorough understanding. A mind that can do this has achieved the desired depth.

A theoretician who is attempting to construct a theory designed to explain a phenomenon has to *prove that her theory is accurate and verified and not just platitudinous*. In order to do so, she has to show how nuanced, comprehensive, critical and detailed her theory is in handling the phenomenon being investigated. This can be achieved only with a thorough investigation of all the underlying concepts and theoretical underpinnings of the problem. A method of conceptual analysis may serve as a great tool in achieving this sort of depth in one's understanding of a problem.

Let us see how we might achieve this sort of depth in our thinking and how we can convince others about the depth of our endeavours.

In our own case

- We should *investigate the underlying structure* of things.
- We should not ignore any lead as irrelevant without making *a thorough enquiry* of it.
- We should be prepared for complexities that may arise during our investigation into the phenomenon under scrutiny.
- We should employ our *analytical ability* to master the complex concepts that are involved in the analysis.

In the case of others

- We should always provide a *detailed analysis* of the problem to our audience before coming up with our own solution.
- We should also present an explanation counter to our own with the same amount of depth and clarity.
- We must *consider the audience's opinion on* the lack of details in our own exposition.

The *human mind finds great comfort in simplicity*. It fights complexities, which poses an intellectual challenge for it. This is why we are often hasty and superficial in our handling of problems. Not only are we too lazy to take on the hard labour associated with a thorough investigation, *we are also afraid of complexities as such*. If an issue has many complex dimensions then we seem to have a fear of losing control over it. This makes us simply shut our eyes to those complexities and gives us a false sense of relief and a superficial sense of control over circumstances. In other words, we deceive ourselves into believing a complex situation is in fact extremely simple.

A critical thinker however can face up to the challenges that are associated with a thorough investigation of a complex issue.

1.3.6 Breadth

The investigation of a problem should not only be deep but also adequately broad. A study has achieved the desired breadth when we have *considered all the relevant aspects*

THINKING THROUGH EXERCISE 7

(i) What is the importance of a comprehensive analysis of a problem?
(ii) How can we ensure that our study of a problem is not superficial?
(iii) How can we achieve depth in our critical thinking?
(iv) What is depth in critical thinking for ourselves and what is it for others?
(v) What are the barriers to achieving depth?

of the problem and have not left any important details unattended. Looking into different aspects of the issue at hand and adopting alternative approaches also helps us achieve the desired breadth. For instance, suppose we want to conduct a survey of TV viewing patterns amongst children aged six to nine years. If we conduct the survey on children only from private schools, our survey results will be narrow as we would have left out a large section of six to nine year olds who do not attend private schools but watch TV. The ability to see a problem from different perspectives is a virtue of the critical mind.

Theoretical investigations also often become narrow because the theoretician is unable to *translate her theory into practice*. An interesting case is that of theoretical ethics. In recent times, grand ethical theories have been criticised for being narrow because they fail to indicate how such theories can have practical applications. In order to change this perception, the field of ethics has now branched off into different kinds of applied ethics, in various areas of practice, like environmental ethics, medical ethics, media ethics, etc.

Let us now see how we may achieve breadth in our thought for ourselves and how can we convince others though it.

In our own case

- ❑ We should at every step ask ourselves whether we have considered all the aspects of the problem at hand.
- ❑ We should at every step try to *think of alternative standpoints* that may be taken on the topic of discussion.
- ❑ We should be as *exhaustive* as possible.

In the case of others

- ❑ We should *encourage our audience to offer an alternative approach* on the issue that we are discussing.
- ❑ We should provide all the relevant details to the audience and be ready to come up with as many *illustrations* and examples as we can.
- ❑ We should also be prepared with *counter examples* that the audience might come up with.

We have now discussed the more important standards of critical thinking. You will find there is yet another standard that is often spoken of by many authorities on critical

KEY POINTS

The following standards or criteria are an indication of critical thinking:

1. Clarity
2. Accuracy
3. Precision
4. Relevance
5. Depth
6. Breadth

THINKING THROUGH EXERCISE 8

(i) In thinking critically, why do we need to achieve breadth in our study?
(ii) How can we achieve breadth in our own case and in the case of others?
(iii) What are the barriers to achieving breadth in our critical thinking?

thinking—logic. We will not discuss this standard here separately. The reason is, all the standards we have discussed so far function and solve problems on the basis of a rational approach guided by logic.

Why does a critical thinker consider accuracy as a standard? It is because truth is a value dear to the logical mind. Why does a critical thinker consider precision and relevance as standards? It is because the logical mind hates ambiguity and imprecision. A logical mind is guided by the diktats of reason and rests only when sufficient evidence supports their convictions. But what is it to be logical in the mind? This is something we shall discuss in this book. But we will specifically discuss core logical issues in the next chapter.

1.4 Critical Thinking: Benefits and Barriers

At the beginning of this chapter, we presented only a broad idea of critical thinking. Let us now consider some *definitions*:

- Critical thinking is reasonable, reflective thinking that is focused on deciding what to believe or do.[3]
- Critical thinking is deciding rationally what to or what not to believe.[4]
- Broadly speaking, critical thinking is concerned with reason, intellectual honesty, and open-mindedness, as opposed to emotionalism, intellectual laziness, and closed-mindedness. Thus, critical thinking involves: following evidence where it leads; considering all possibilities; relying on reason rather than emotion; being precise; considering a variety of possible viewpoints and explanations; weighing the effects of motives and biases; being concerned more with finding the truth than with being right; not rejecting unpopular views out of hand; being aware of one's own prejudices and biases, and not allowing them to sway one's judgment.[5]

All these definitions reiterate what we read at the beginning of this chapter: critical thinking makes us intellectually responsible adults. It enables us to:

- reflect (become rational)
- follow certain standards of reflective thinking (exercise good, rational judgement)
- think through things for ourselves (have a sense of rational responsibility)
- be reasonable (be fair)
- believe or do things on the basis of reason rather than emotion or prejudices (be open-minded)

How do we actually do all this?

- We start off by developing a questioning attitude.
- We remember that this questioning attitude is as much self-directed as it is other-directed. Hence, we have to be self-critical. This does not make us weak and diffident but helps us gear up for the challenges that come in the form of criticism from others.
- We test each belief on the basis of available evidence and judge if what we believe rationally follows from the evidence we have.
- We only form beliefs that we are ready to defend with the help of reason.
- When we are to examine a problem, we:

  "**S** State the problem

  E Elaborate it (i.e., explain it more thoroughly in our own words)

  E Exemplify (i.e., provide a good example)

  I Illustrate (i.e., provide an illustration—a metaphor, a simile, an analogy, a diagram, a concept map, etc.)"[6]

A person with good critical thinking skills is blessed with a rare quality. Many people are intelligent but those who are trained in critical thinking have the rare quality of being intellectually responsible. This means they are fair, reasonable, rationally and intellectually self-sufficient, not easily corrupted, not easily brain-washed, more or less free from biases and prejudices and able to take the right decisions all by themselves by making the right kind of evaluation of a circumstance. Here, we may quote from William Graham Sumner's *Folkways: A Study of the Sociological Importance of Usages, Manners, Customs, Mores, and Morals*:

> The critical habit of thought, if usual in society, will pervade all its mores, because it is a way of taking up problems of life. Men educated in it cannot be stampeded by stump orators ... They are slow to believe. They can hold things as possible or probable in all degrees, without certainty and without pain. They can wait for evidence and weigh evidence, uninfluenced by the emphasis or confidence with which assertions are made on one side or the other. They can resist the appeal to their dearest prejudices and all kinds of cajolery. Education in critical faculty is the only education of which it can be truly said that it makes good citizens.[7]

There are great *academic benefits* of critical thinking. Suppose you are teaching students a course on chemistry. This course would have two aspects—the first is of course the subject matter of the course and the second is teaching the students the correct way in which to evaluate and understand the subject matter. It is this second aspect that is addressed by critical thinking. As critical thinking teaches you *how to think*, once you are skilled in critical thinking, you are able to learn whatever you are taught in the most judicious way, no matter what the subject being taught—chemistry, English literature, information technology, or commerce.

Critical thinking thus helps students to *improve their academic performance*. This is achieved by the exercise of the skills associated with critical thinking, which we have described while mentioning the standards of critical thinking. Critical thinkers are clear, accurate, precise and able to hold views that are relevant, adequately deep, broad and logical. Being so logical, we are not only able to become smart enquirers but also people with a special strength of mind—a mind that is free from bias and prejudices and is liberal and not easily over-powered by cunning cajoling or befooled by clever deceit.

The *barriers* to critical reasoning are many as is clear from our discussion of the barriers to achieving the standards of critical reasoning. There are some more serious barriers to critical thinking that are sociological and psychological in nature. A thorough understanding of these barriers requires a certain amount of background knowledge. We can however mention a few of them in brief. Do remember that there are many others.

Social brainwashing and our view of the world: A critical thinker is a person who is trying to work her way through the world in a reflective way. In doing so, she is required to have some sort of understanding of the world around her. But the question is, how does she form her view of the world? Usually, our views about our surroundings are initially influenced by our parents' views. However, they are not always able to give us a full or unbiased picture of the world. Later in life, our views are shaped by our role models such as our teachers, by our peers or even by celebrities like film stars whose fans we are. But the most serious and profound influence on our view of the world is exercised by the media, both print and electronic. What we believe about the world we live in is to a very large extent directed by newspapers and news channels. This hidden control over our thoughts has hindered a free and reflecting thought process. This is possibly the greatest barrier to free critical thinking.

Tendency to think in binaries: We usually think in binaries, i.e., bad or good, just or unjust, we or they, liberal or conservative, black or white, absolute or relative, objective or subjective. Thinking in binaries is not only common to the common man, it is a thought pattern so deeply embedded in us that it affects even the most famous and astute logician, philosopher, political thinker or scientist. But the world and all the worldly phenomena that we encounter are not all to be judged in terms of binaries. This has not only led to poor theories in the field of philosophy but also to the breakdown of personal relations. Being a critical thinker is hard for those who follow the stereotype that defines this thinking in terms of binaries.

Fears regarding freethinking: We often toe the line set by others in spite of realising in our minds that they are wrong. We do this because we are scared to be the first to voice a new opinion. This fear stems from our fear of making mistakes, the fear of making a fool of ourselves. This is the result of a kind of intellectual diffidence. This diffidence may have some sociological roots as many societies discourage freethinking. Our educational system, which has an ingrained patronising spirit, also discourages freethinking. A free thinker therefore can feel cornered and will need an enormously strong will to come out and say what she thinks is right.

Egocentrism: Most people think that they are the centre of the universe. Some people are even full blown megalomaniacs. Even still, everything that we see we see from our own perspective. In a way, this is the only perspective we have. But to be a critical thinker, we need to go beyond our own perspective and be able to appreciate other ways of looking at things.

KEY POINTS

- Critical thinking has immense benefits. It makes us intellectually responsible adults.
- There are, however, numerous barriers to critical thinking. Some of these are:
  1. Social brainwashing
  2. Tendency to think in binaries
  3. Fears regarding freethinking
  4. Egocentrism
  5. Personal interests and experiences

THINKING THROUGH EXERCISE 9

(i) Can you try to define critical thinking?
(ii) What are the achievements of a critical thinker?
(iii) What does a critical thinker need to do in order to succeed?
(iv) What are the benefits of critical thinking?
(v) What are the barriers to critical thinking?

Personal interests and experiences: In our lives, we have many a commitment that steers the direction of the path we take. Our past experiences determine our allegiances, our emotional and social commitments. It is difficult to answer the call of reason in the face of the tremendous pressure that our past experiences and commitments place upon us.

1.5 Concluding Remarks

We have seen above what critical thinking is and what we need to do if we are to be critical thinkers. I would like to highlight a few things that we have learnt from this discussion:

- Critical thinking is all about being intellectually responsible.
- Critical thinking involves employing one's reason and always keeping in view certain standards of good and effective thinking.
- Critical thinking enables us to effectively handle questions about the world around us (known as empirical questions).
- Critical thinking involves the recognition and evaluation of inferences and arguments.

- Critical thinking enables us to differentiate between the relevant and the irrelevant.
- Critical thinking helps us increase our knowledge by taking us beyond the information that is given to us.
- Critical thinking involves realising how important the context of a phenomenon is in order to explain it.
- Critical thinking is directed towards explanation, understanding, testing and prediction.
- Critical thinking depends upon feedback from others for its success.
- Critical thinking is also the art of persuasion.
- Critical thinking helps us overcome various biases that hinder freethinking.
- Critical thinking helps us recognise fallacies in our thoughts. It also teaches us how to build certain safeguards against fallacious thinking.
- Critical thinking makes us aware and sensitive to emotions and needs.

1.6 More Exercises

1. Story

Rakesh and Anjali were planning to buy a flat. On their way back from office one day, they saw an advertisement for a housing complex. They called up the contact person who asked them to come over to the site to see if they liked the project. It was a beautiful flat on a beautiful site but miles away from their office and miles away from their children's school. It was also a little beyond their budget, but it was so wonderful that they decided to take a housing loan and buy it. In a few months, they bought it and moved in. But now they are miserable.

Exercise

Why do you think Rakesh and Anjali are miserable? What are the things that they should have considered before buying the flat? What could they have done to avoid this misery? What are the critical thinking standards that they failed to meet?

2. Story

The Red-Headed League *by Arthur Conan Doyle*

I had called upon my friend, Mr Sherlock Holmes, one day in the autumn of last year and found him in deep conversation with a very stout, florid-faced, elderly gentleman with fiery red hair. With an apology for my intrusion, I was about to withdraw when Holmes pulled me abruptly into the room and closed the door behind me.

"You could not possibly have come at a better time, my dear Watson," he said cordially.

"I was afraid that you were engaged."

"So I am. Very much so."

"Then I can wait in the next room."

"Not at all. This gentleman, Mr Wilson, has been my partner and helper in many of my most successful cases, and I have no doubt that he will be of the utmost use to me in yours also."

The stout gentleman half rose from his chair and gave a bob of greeting, with a quick little questioning glance from his small, fat-encircled eyes.

"Try the settee," said Holmes, relapsing into his armchair, and putting his fingertips together, as was his custom when in judicial moods. "I know, my dear Watson, that you share my love of all that is bizarre and outside the conventions and humdrum routine of everyday life. You have shown your relish for it by the enthusiasm which has prompted you to chronicle, and, if you will excuse my saying so, somewhat to embellish so many of my own little adventures."

"Your cases have indeed been of the greatest interest to me," I observed.

"You will remember that I remarked the other day, just before we went into the very simple problem presented by Miss Mary Sutherland, that for strange effects and extraordinary combinations we must go to life itself, which is always far more daring than any effort of the imagination."

"A proposition which I took the liberty of doubting."

"You did, Doctor, but none the less you must come round to my view, for otherwise I shall keep on piling fact upon fact on you until your reason breaks down under them and acknowledges me to be right. Now, Mr Jabez Wilson here has been good enough to call upon me this morning, and to begin a narrative which promises to be one of the most singular which I have listened to for some time. You have heard me remark that the strangest and most unique things are very often connected not with the larger but with the smaller crimes, and occasionally, indeed, where there is room for doubt whether any positive crime has been committed. As far as I have heard it is impossible for me to say whether the present case is an instance of crime or not, but the course of events is certainly among the most singular that I have ever listened to. Perhaps, Mr. Wilson, you would have the great kindness to recommence your narrative. I ask you not merely because my friend Dr. Watson has not heard the opening part, but also because the peculiar nature of the story makes me anxious to have every possible detail from your lips. As a rule, when I have heard some slight indication of the course of events, I am able to guide myself by the thousands of other similar cases which occur to my memory. In the present instance I am forced to admit that the facts are, to the best of my belief, unique."

The portly client puffed out his chest with an appearance of some little pride and pulled a dirty and wrinkled newspaper from the inside pocket of his greatcoat. As he glanced down the advertisement column, with his head thrust forward, and the paper flattened out upon his knee, I took a good look at the man and endeavoured, after the fashion of my companion, to read the indications which might be presented by his dress or appearance.

I did not gain very much, however, by my inspection. Our visitor bore every mark of being an average commonplace British tradesman, obese, pompous, and slow. He wore rather baggy grey shepherd's check trousers, a not over clean black frockcoat, unbuttoned in the front, and a drab waistcoat with a heavy brassy Albert chain, and a square pierced bit of metal dangling down as an ornament. A frayed top hat and a faded brown overcoat with a wrinkled velvet collar lay upon a chair beside him. Altogether, look as I would, there was nothing remarkable about the man save his blazing red head, and the expression of extreme chagrin and discontent upon his features.

Sherlock Holmes' quick eye took in my occupation, and he shook his head with a smile as he noticed my questioning glances. "Beyond the obvious facts that he has at some time done manual labour, that he takes snuff, that he is a Freemason, that he has been in China, and that he has done a considerable amount of writing lately, I can deduce nothing else."

Mr. Jabez Wilson started up in his chair, with his forefinger upon the paper, but his eyes upon my companion.

"How, in the name of good fortune, did you know all that, Mr Holmes?" he asked. "How did you know, for example, that I did manual labour? It's as true as gospel, for I began as a ship's carpenter."

"Your hands, my dear sir. Your right hand is quite a size larger than your left. You have worked with it, and the muscles are more developed."

"Well, the snuff, then, and the Freemasonry?"

"I won't insult your intelligence by telling you how I read that, especially as, rather against the strict rules of your order, you use an arc and compass breastpin."

"Ah, of course, I forgot that. But the writing?"

"What else can be indicated by that right cuff so very shiny for five inches, and the left one with the smooth patch near the elbow where you rest it upon the desk?"

"Well, but China?"

"The fish that you have tattooed immediately above your right wrist could only have been done in China. I have made a small study of tattoo marks, and have even contributed to the literature of the subject. That trick of staining the fishes' scales of a delicate pink is quite peculiar to China. When, in addition, I see a Chinese coin hanging from your watch-chain, the matter becomes even more simple."

Mr. Jabez Wilson laughed heavily. "Well, I never!" said he. "I thought at first that you had done something clever, but I see that there was nothing in it after all."

Exercise

What has Sherlock Holmes achieved? What are the relevant standards of critical thinking that he has applied in the story above?

3. Conversation

Rehana: *Don't smoke, Akash, or else you will get lung cancer.*
Akash: *What makes you think so?*
Rehana: *They say so in the newspapers.*

Akash: *My aunt never smoked a single cigarette but she had lung cancer.*
Rehana: *Whatever is written in the newspapers is true.*
Akash: *Then why did my aunt have lung cancer?*

Exercise

Evaluate Rehana and Akash's statements and questions and determine which standards of critical thinking they have failed to meet.

4. Conversation

Varun: *Where are you going, Mother?*
Mother: *Outside.*
Varun: *I can see that!*

Exercise

What is the standard of critical thinking that Varun's mother fails to fulfil?

5. Conversation

Ranjan: *The MLA should not have said that only criminals of a particular community were being caught by the police.*
Rajam: *Why not? He has the right to speech.*
Ranjan: *But the law is that one should not publicly make a statement that hurts the sentiment of a particular community.*

Exercise

Evaluate this debate keeping in mind the standards of critical thinking.

6. Conversation

Ben: *Why have you given me cereal with my milk? You know I hate it!*
Mother: *Have a look at the packet. It says that a bowl of this cereal with milk will give you 25 per cent of the daily amount of protein recommended by physicians.*
Ben: *Does the protein come from the cereal or the milk?*

Exercise

Who is thinking critically here? Justify your answer.

7. Conversation

Mother: *You should now think of getting married.*
Tulika: *Why?*
Mother: *Why not? You are 25 years old now.*
Tulika: *Have you thought about whether this is the right time for me to get married?*

Mother: But I said you should get married because you are 25.
Tulika: *Is age the only factor in deciding if it is the right time to get married?*
Mother: *What else should it be?*

Exercise

Can you answer Mother's question on Tulika's behalf keeping in mind all the standards and barriers to critical thinking?

NOTES AND REFERENCES

1. Plato, *Apology* (Harmondsworth: Penguin, 1969), 38a, p. 72.

2. Gerald M. Nosich, *Learning to Think Things Through* (Upper Saddle River, NJ: Pearson, Prentice Hall, 2009).

3. Robert Ennis, "A taxonomy of critical thinking skills and dispositions," in Baron and Sternberg (eds.) *Teaching Thinking Skills: Theory and Practice* (New York, NY: Freeman, 1987).

4. S. P Norris, "Synthesis of Research on Critical Thinking," *Educational Leadership*, vol. 42, no. 8, May 1985, pp 40–45.

5. Daniel J. Kurland, *I Know What It Says … What Does It Mean?* (Florence, KY: Wadsworth Publishing, 1995).

6. Ibid., p. 34.

7. William Graham Sumner, *Folkways: A Study of the Sociological Importance of Usages, Manners, Customs, Mores, and Morals* (New York, NY: Ginn and Co.1940).

2

CRITICAL THINKING AND LOGIC

Histories make men wise; poets, witty; the mathematics, subtle; natural philosophy, deep; moral, grave; logic and rhetoric, able to contend.

—*Francis Bacon*

2.1 Introduction

Critical thinking is often also called *informal logic*. The central theme of critical thinking is logic and all that is relevant to logic. Informal logic is often contrasted with what is known as *formal logic*. But before we analyse the distinction between these two kinds of logic, we need get a general understanding of what logic is.

Logic can be described as the systematic study of inferences. The British empiricist philosopher John Locke once said, "Logic is the anatomy of thought". Formal logic is the study of the form of inferences or arguments, which enables us to judge whether an argument has a form that has been recognised as a form of proper inference, wherein the conclusion is derived from the premises following certain accepted rules or methods of inference. Although informal logic is not so concerned with the formalisation that defines formal logic, it helps to assess inferences without being involved with formalisation. If we look into the history of informal logic, we will see that it developed as a discipline simply to enable us to "assess, analyse and improve ordinary language (or 'everyday') reasoning".[1]

We must remember that critical thinking and informal logic is an interdisciplinary approach to inferences or arguments. This is so because an attempt to understand reasoning is made in critical thinking from the "point of view of philosophy, formal logic, cognitive psychology, and a range of other disciplines. Most of the work in informal logic focuses on the reasoning and argument (in the premise-conclusion sense) one finds in personal exchange, advertising, political debate, legal argument, and the social commentary that characterises newspapers, television, the World Wide Web, and other forms of mass media".[2] What is clear by now is that *in critical thinking we are concerned with inferences or arguments*. It is in this respect that critical thinking is related with logic and especially with *arguments—their recognition and their evaluation*. We shall start with the recognition of an argument.

2.2 What Is an Argument?

In a very general way, we may say that whenever a person gives *reasons in order to support a claim*, she is attempting at presenting an argument. "To attempt to persuade by giving good reasons is to give an argument."[3] Such arguments are found in great abundance, not only in the works of great philosophers or logicians but also in everyday discourse. We are always presenting our friends, our families and our work mates with numerous arguments in support of what we believe, what we do and what we think. Whenever there is a controversy or debate about some issue, we find contenders in the debate presenting arguments either to resolve or dissolve the debate or sometimes to keep the debate alive. We have to remember that *an argument is always backed by reason or evidence*. In this respect, an argument is different from its close neighbour, *opinion*.

Consider the following claims:

- The BJP was doing a better job running the country than the Congress Party is doing now.
- All children of parents who speak different languages are dyslexics.
- Logicians are humourless people.

We would surely understand that these are opinions and not arguments. But the statements below are most certainly arguments:

- The BJP was doing a better job running the country than the Congress Party is doing now because during their tenure there was lesser unemployment and the inflation was also lower.
- In the past, I have met nearly ten children whose parents speak different languages and all of them were dyslexics. So all children of parents who speak different languages are dyslexics.
- Logicians are constantly engaged in exercises of reason, in which there is no place for emotion. An emotionless person is incapable of humour. So all logicians are humourless.

All these are possibly bad arguments but they are arguments nonetheless and cannot be regarded as mere opinions like the previous set. We should be able to understand that an *unsupported opinion* or *a mere description* cannot be regarded as an argument. For instance, if I say, "It was a hot and humid April morning, and I was desperately trying to finish the second chapter of my book on critical thinking," then neither would I be voicing an opinion, nor expressing an argument. What I am doing here is just describing an April morning. Suppose you say, "How many people in Chennai read *The Times of India*?" I would be asking a question. So not everything that we say, hear, write or read are arguments.

We need to remember that we may come to form opinions by following a course of rational deliberation. In such a case, our opinions are based on arguments, which in turn are based on reasons or evidence. But we must also remember that not all opinions are backed by arguments. If we look at opinions from a political point of view, we may claim that every individual has the right to his or her opinion. But we need to remember that from a logical point of view, all opinions are not at par. One might just arrive at an opinion following one's own gut feeling. This is definitely different from an opinion that has resulted from a long and reasoned thought process.

What critical thinking teaches is to form opinions on the basis of evidence and arguments because opinions on serious and controversial matters have to be defended by rational arguments. It is in this sense that critical thinking really liberates people as it makes them judge what they are told to do and believe and also helps them think through all these before arriving at an opinion or taking a course of action. But how do we recognise an argument?

KEY POINTS

What is and what is not an argument?

- To attempt to persuade by giving good reasons is to present an argument.
- Whatever counts as an argument is always backed by reason or evidence.
- It is wrong to regard an argument as an opinion when it is not supported by any evidence.
- An argument is not a mere description.
- What critical thinking teaches you to do is to form opinions on the basis of evidence and arguments because opinions on serious and controversial matters have to be defended by rational arguments.

THINKING THROUGH EXERCISE 1

i. When do we present arguments?
ii. Can you provide examples of arguments and opinions?
iii. How does a description differ from an argument?
iv. Are all opinions irrational?
v. How does knowledge of arguments help us become good critical thinkers?

2.3 How Can We Recognise an Argument?

An argument is a *string of connected statements* of which some are *premises* on the basis of which one of them i.e., the *conclusion*, is established. The premises may be regarded as the set of claims that a person puts forward in order to support a further claim that she wants to make, which is the conclusion. In plain language, we may say that *every argument has two parts*: The *principal claim* the argument is trying to persuade us to accept is the *conclusion*. The others (there may also be just one) are the claims that *support* the primary claim by *providing reasons* for accepting it and these are the *premises*. Let us try to illustrate through an example what we have discussed so far:

All Kathakali dancers are from Kerala.
Raghu is a Kathakali dancer.
So, Raghu is from Kerala.

Note:

- Here, the *principal claim* is that Raghu is from Kerala
- So the *conclusion* is that Raghu is from Kerala
- In order to support this claim, two other *supporting claims* are made from which the conclusion follows. These are premises.
- The *premises* are:
  i. All Kathakali dancers are from Kerala
  ii. Raghu is a Kathakali dancer

We need to remember a few things here. We can have even just one premise in an argument. Not all arguments need more premises than that. Let us consider an example:

No foreigners are allowed to vote in the national elections.

Therefore, no one who is allowed to vote in the national election can be a foreigner.

Note:

- Here, the *principal claim* is that no one who is allowed to vote in the national elections can be a foreigner.
- So the *conclusion* is that no one who is allowed to vote in the national election can be a foreigner.
- In order to support this claim, only one *supporting claim* is made from which the conclusion follows. This is the *premise*.
- The *premise* is:
  No foreigners are allowed to vote in the national elections

We may now try to understand how we can recognise an argument. We should look for the following features in an argument:

- A string of statements
- Relation between these statements

KEY POINTS

What is an argument? How can we recognise it?

- ❑ An argument is a string of connected statements of which some are premises on the basis of which one of them, i.e., the conclusion, is established.
- ❑ The conclusion is the principal claim of the argument.
- ❑ The other claims that support the principal claim are premises.
- ❑ We may recognise an argument by:
  - i. finding a string of statements
  - ii. determining if the statements in the strings are related
  - iii. determining if the relation is such that some of the statements support one of the statements, which is the principal claim
  - iv. finding the supporting statements that are the premises
  - v. finding the supported statement that is the conclusion.

THINKING THROUGH EXERCISE 2

i. What is an argument?
ii. What are the principal claims of an argument and what are the supporting claims of an argument?
iii. How do you recognise an argument?

- ❑ The relation should be such that some of the statements support one of the statements (the supporting statements are premises).
- ❑ The supported statement, which is the conclusion, should follow words like "therefore" and "so".

A thorough understanding of the flow of an argument depends upon our recognition of premises and the conclusion. Let us now see how that can be done.

2.4 Premises, Hidden Premises, Conclusions, and Intermediate Conclusions

We have discussed what a premise is and also what a conclusion is. There are certain words that may be regarded as *indicator words* for premises and conclusions. These indicator words not only indicate that an argument is being presented but also indicate which of the statements in the argument are premises and which are conclusions. Let us see what these indicator words may be.[4]

Indicator words for premises

- ❑ since
- ❑ it follows from
- ❑ is established by the fact that
- ❑ because
- ❑ as is indicated by
- ❑ is implied by
- ❑ for
- ❑ given that

Indicator words for conclusions

- ❑ therefore
- ❑ hence
- ❑ in conclusion
- ❑ as a result
- ❑ establishes
- ❑ thus
- ❑ it follows that
- ❑ accordingly
- ❑ implies
- ❑ so
- ❑ then
- ❑ consequently
- ❑ shows

We may now try to make use of our knowledge of these indicator words to determine the premise and the conclusion of an argument. We shall consider rather complicated arguments and see how indicator words come handy in deciphering their structure. Here is one example:

> *There is life somewhere in the universe as well as here on earth, for the universe is infinite and it can't be that in an infinite universe only one place has the special features needed for life.*[5]

If we look carefully into this argument, we will notice a few things:

- ❑ Though we usually think that the conclusion comes at the end and is followed by the words or phrases that are indicators of conclusions, in this case it is mentioned right at the beginning and has no conclusion indicating phrase attached to it.
- ❑ The conclusion is: *There is life somewhere in the universe as well as here on earth.*
- ❑ We know this because there is a premise indicator that differentiates the premises from the conclusion. The premise indicator is the word "for".
- ❑ What follows after the word *"for"* are premises.
- ❑ The premises are:
  - *i. The universe is infinite.*
  - *ii. It can't be that in an infinite universe only one place has the special features needed for life.*

We may now rewrite the argument in the following way:

> *Premise 1: The universe is infinite.*
> *Premise 2: It can't be that in an infinite universe only one place has the special features needed for life.*
> *Conclusion: There is life somewhere in the universe as well as here on earth.*

Let us consider another argument:

If Susan is leaving for New Delhi early tomorrow morning then she will be back home by 8.
She is back home by 8.
So, she must be leaving for New Delhi early tomorrow morning.

If we look carefully into the argument, we will notice:

- There is a conclusion indicator in the argument, i.e., the word *so*.
- The conclusion is: *Susan must be leaving for New Delhi early tomorrow morning.*
- The rest of the statements of the argument are premises.
- The premises are:
  - *i. If Susan is leaving for New Delhi early tomorrow morning then she will be back home by 8.*
  - *ii. Susan is back home by 8.*

We may now rewrite the argument is the following way:

Premise 1: If Susan is leaving for New Delhi early tomorrow morning then she will be back home by 8.
Premise 2: Susan is back home by 8.
Conclusion: Therefore, Susan must be leaving for New Delhi early tomorrow morning.

KEY POINTS

- We should look for words indicating the premises.
- We should look for words indicating the conclusion.
- Not all arguments are organized in the same manner.

THINKING THROUGH EXERCISE 3

i. What are the two things that we need to recognise in order to recognise an argument?
ii. What are premise indicators?
iii. What are conclusion indicators?
iv. Do arguments have to be organised in the same manner? Give examples to illustrate your answer.

2.5 Hidden Premises

We shall now discuss some arguments that have hidden premises. These are known as enthymemes. Consider an argument of the following kind:

> *Premise: It's morally wrong to treat human beings as mere objects.*
> *Conclusion: So, genetically engineering human beings is morally wrong.*[6]

We may think that this is an argument with just one premise. This however is not true. If we notice carefully, we will realise that there is a hidden premise lurking here:

> *If we genetically engineer human beings then we would be treating them as mere objects.*

We may consider another example:

> *Premise: It is our moral duty to provide food for future generations.*
> *Conclusion: It follows that it is our moral duty to genetically engineer crops.*[7]

We must realise that the hidden premise in this case is:

> *Genetically engineering crops provides food for future generations.*

Here, we are finding out the inner connection that validates the connection being made in the conclusion. In the conclusion of this particular argument, what is being stated is that *it is our moral duty to harvest genetically engineered crops*. At first, it might seem strange to you for this claim to be supported by the premise, "*it is our moral duty to provide food for future generations*". But soon we realise that the only possible way that this can be achieved is by genetically engineering crops, and that is why the premise we already have might be regarded as a support for the conclusion. So we provide the hidden premise: *Genetically engineering crops provides food for future generations.*

Let us consider another simple example from everyday conversation. Suppose you say to a friend, "Amitabh Bachchan is taller than Shah Rukh Khan," and the friend at once responds, "Oh! Then he has to be taller than Aamir Khan too." What is clear at once to us is that your friend is saying this because he already knows that Shah Rukh Khan is taller than Aamir Khan. And this is the hidden premise that supports his conclusion that Amitabh Bachchan is taller than Aamir Khan.

KEY POINTS

Hidden premises

- ❑ Not all premises of an argument are spelt out in an argument.
- ❑ We must find the hidden premise by trying to identify the missing relating statement that can relate the given premise with the conclusion.

THINKING THROUGH EXERCISE 4

i. What is a hidden premise?
ii. Give two examples of arguments with hidden premises.

2.6 Intermediate Conclusions

Sometimes we have arguments that contain intermediate conclusions. Intermediate conclusions work as premises of a subsequent argument that occurs within the body of the original argument itself. Let us consider an example:

Sher Khan is a tiger.
All tigers are carnivorous.
So Sher Khan is also carnivorous.
And since all carnivorous animals have sharp teeth, Sher Khan too has sharp teeth.

Now let us re-write this argument with the intermediate conclusion clearly specified.

Premise 1: Sher Khan is a tiger
Premise 2: All tigers are carnivorous.
Conclusion 1 and Premise 3: Sher Khan is carnivorous.
Premise 4: All carnivorous animals have sharp teeth.
Conclusion 2: Sher Khan too has sharp teeth.

Notice that Conclusion 1 follows from Premises 1 and 2. Then Conclusion 1 doubles up as Premise 3, which along with Premise 4 leads to Conclusion 2. So here the *intermediate conclusion* is that *Sher Khan is carnivorous.*

We may consider another argument that has within it a sub-argument:

A computer cannot cheat in a game, because cheating means deliberately breaking rules in order to win. A computer cannot deliberately break rules because it has no freedom of action.[8]

Now let us re-write this argument.

Premise 1: A computer has no freedom of action.
Conclusion 1 and Premise 2: Thus, a computer cannot deliberately break rules.
Premise 3: Cheating requires deliberate breaking of rules.
Conclusion 2: Therefore, a computer cannot cheat.

Note here we have an argument that contains another sub-argument. And the *intermediate conclusion*, "A computer cannot deliberately break rules," serves as a premise for the principal conclusion, "A computer cannot cheat".

KEY POINTS

Intermediate conclusions

- ❑ Many arguments contain a sub-argument.
- ❑ The conclusion of the sub-argument serves as a premise for the entire argument.
- ❑ These conclusions are regarded as intermediate conclusions.

THINKING THROUGH EXERCISE 5

i. What is an intermediate conclusion?

ii. How does a statement perform the dual role of a premise as well as a conclusion?

iii. Give two examples of arguments that have intermediate conclusions.

2.7 Truth Content and Logical Content

We shall now be discussing an extremely important feature of logical arguments. When we are trying to understand what an argument is, we realise that it is an attempt at establishing a claim on the basis of other claims. If I present an argument for Claim A by supporting it with Claim B and Claim C, then what I am saying is that if you accept Claims B and C then you have to also accept Claim A. I say this because Claim A follows from Claims B and C. It is as if Claim A is *hidden inside* Claim B and Claim C, and all we do in the argument is bring it out. We have to remember that at no point are we claiming that either Claim A, B or C are actually true. Consider this argument:

Raj Kapoor is the father of Shekhar Kapoor.
Shekhar Kapoor is the father of Anil Kapoor.
So, Raj Kapoor is the grandfather of Anil Kapoor.

Notice that this is an extremely good argument though both of its premises as well as its conclusion are false. But the falsity of the premises or the conclusion does not make the argument in question a bad argument.

We need to realise that in logic, we are interested in two things:

i. The *truth content* of a statement

ii. The logical content of a statement

On the one hand, in the case of the statement "Raj Kapoor is the father of Shekhar Kapoor," we may ask whether it is factually true. In such a case, we would be trying to evaluate the evidence that we need to establish the truth of this statement. So we would be concerned with the *truth content* of the statement. On the other hand, in the case of the statement "Raj Kapoor is the father of Shekhar Kapoor," we might ask what would follow

KEY POINTS

Truth content and logical content

- When we are asking for evidence for the truth of any of the statements of an argument, we are asking about the truth content of the argument.
- When we are asking whether the conclusion follows from the premises, we are asking about the logical content of an argument.
- In evaluating the logical content of an argument, the relevant concept is validity.

THINKING THROUGH EXERCISE 6

i. What is the truth content of an argument?
ii. What is the logical content of an argument?
iii. Provide some examples of arguments that have the same logical content but different truth content.

from it if it were true. In the above argument, we realise that if both the premises were true then whatever would follow from it would be the conclusion. In such a case, we are concerned with the *logical content* of the statement.

When evaluating an argument, we have to take into account both the truth content and the logical content. We must understand that there may be flaws in arguments both due to errors in truth content or errors in logical content. When there is some error in logical content, we are left with an argument that is *invalid*. We are now going to discuss one of the most, if not the most, important concept in logic—*validity*.

2.8 Validity

We are going to once again consider our argument with false premises and a false conclusion:

Argument 1
Raj Kapoor is the father of Shekhar Kapoor.
Shekhar Kapoor is the father of Anil Kapoor.
So, Raj Kapoor is the grandfather of Anil Kapoor.

Consider another argument that is exactly like this but with a few changes in the names:

Argument 2
Raj Kapoor is the father of Randhir Kapoor.
Randhir Kapoor is the father of Karishma Kapoor.
So, Raj Kapoor is the grandfather of Karishma Kapoor.

Now we have an argument exactly like the previous one but all the statements involved in this argument (both the premises and the conclusion) are true. Consider another argument very much like the two above:

Argument 3
Raj Kapoor is the father of Shekhar Kapoor.
Shekhar Kapoor is the father of Karishma Kapoor.
So, Raj Kapoor is the grandfather of Karishma Kapoor.

Now we have an argument that has two false premises but has a true conclusion. Consider another argument quite like these:

Argument 4
Raj Kapoor is the father of Pankaj Kapoor.
Pankaj Kapoor is the father of Shahid Kapoor.
So, Raj Kapoor is the grandfather of Shahid Kapoor.

Here we have an argument with one false premise and a false conclusion. What is interesting is that we would never be able to find an argument of the same kind with two true premises and a false conclusion. We already have Argument 2, which is also an argument with two true premises but not a false conclusion. So let us see if we can construct such an argument. To begin with, we need to understand what makes all these arguments similar. The similarity lies in the pattern, which is roughly as follows:

X is the father of Y.
Y is the father of Z.
So, X is the grandfather of Z.

We can arrive at all the possible categories of arguments simply by replacing the terms X, Y and Z. Let us now consider an argument of the above pattern in which two premises are true.

Prithviraj Kapoor is the father of Raj Kapoor.
Raj Kapoor is the father of Rishi Kapoor.

Here we have two premises that are true and are of the pattern:

X is the father of Y.
Y is the father of Z.

Just blindly following the pattern of arriving at the conclusion, we will arrive at the following:

Prithviraj Kapoor is the grandfather of Rishi Kapoor.

To our surprise, we shall see that this conclusion is true. We can continue like this and we will see in each case that true premises will lead to true conclusions. Why is this? The answer is simple: If X is the father of Y and if Y is the father of Z then X has to be the grandfather of Z. Such is the relation between a grandfather and a grandchild. Here, X is

KEY POINTS

Validity

- An argument is valid if it is impossible for its conclusion to be false when the premises are true
- A valid argument might well contain false statements
- Arguments wherein the truth of the premises definitely leads to a truthful conclusion are deductive arguments

THINKING THROUGH EXERCISE 7

i. When is an argument valid?
ii. Can an argument that has all false statements be valid?
iii. Provide an example of an argument with one false premise and a true conclusion.

the grandfather of Z if he is Z's father's father. So we see that there is something inherent in the pattern of this argument that ensures that if an argument with this pattern has two true premises then its conclusion will definitely be true. This is a *valid* argument.

In the case of any *valid argument*, it is impossible for the premises to be true but the conclusion false. Validity ensures that in an argument, we move from truth to truth. This is so because when one presents an argument, one is saying, "If you accept my premises, that is, if my premises are true, then you will have to accept my conclusion, that is, the conclusion will also be true". This statement captures the essence of the notion of validity.

We must now come to an even more important point. The arguments we have been discussing are known as *deductive arguments*—arguments wherein the truth of the premises ensures the truth of the conclusion. The notion of a deductive argument and validity are closely tied. We shall now discuss these two concepts.

2.9 Deductive Arguments and Validity

From what we have discussed already, we must understand that a deductive argument is "an inference in which it is asserted that the conclusion is guaranteed to be true if the premises are true".[9] Deductive arguments have two important features:

i. In a deductive argument, there is a strict relation between the premises and the conclusion. The relation is strict in the sense that it is impossible for the conclusion to be false if the premises are true. This is so because the conclusion is in fact contained within the premises. In a way, in a deductive argument, the conclusion cannot and does not go beyond the premises and so it is impossible for it to turn out false when the premises are true. This is why the premises strictly guarantee the truth of the conclusion. It is not as though they make the conclusion probable—they make it certain.

ii. There is something in the very pattern (or, as it is termed in the study of logic, the *form*) of a deductive argument that ensures its validity.

Let us now consider a deductive argument and verify the existence of these two features. We begin with choosing our second argument from the previous section:

Raj Kapoor is the father of Randhir Kapoor.
Randhir Kapoor is the father of Karishma Kapoor.
So, Raj Kapoor is the grandfather of Karishma Kapoor.

Let us see how the first feature is present in this argument. The first premise is that Raj Kapoor is Randhir Kapoor's father, and the second premise is that Randhir Kapoor is Karishma Kapoor's father. So what we are saying is that Raj Kapoor is Karishma Kapoor's father's father i.e., her grandfather. Isn't that what the conclusion is saying? This truly shows that the conclusion does not go beyond the premises of the argument and so it is impossible for it to turn out false when the premises are true. This is why the premises strictly guarantee the truth of the conclusion.

Let us now see how the second feature is present in this argument. We have already examined in the previous section how the pattern of this argument forbids the formation of an argument that has the same pattern or *form* and premises that are true but a conclusion that is false. This point can be made clearer by considering another argument:

If Kolkata Knight Riders win the IPL then Shah Rukh Khan will be happy.
Kolkata Knight Riders won the IPL.
So, Shah Rukh Khan is happy.

We will first try to see what the pattern or the form of the argument is:

If X, then Y.
X.
So, Y.

We can see that this is a valid argument. It will be impossible for us to come up with a premise with the form *If X then Y* and another premise *X*, both of which are true, leading to a conclusion with the form *Y* that is not true. For example:

If Kolkata is more densely populated than Chennai then it is more densely populated than Agra.
Kolkata is more densely populated than Chennai.
So, Kolkata is more densely populated than Agra.

We shall see that even in this argument the two premises contain the conclusion and so this conclusion does not really go beyond the premises. We also see that the form of the argument ensures its validity. We must mention here that if a deductive argument is not only valid but also has true premises and conclusions then the argument is *sound*. We must also mention that the kind of arguments we find in geometry are deductive in nature.

KEY POINTS

Deductive arguments and validity

- A deductive argument is an inference in which it is asserted that the conclusion is guaranteed to be true if the premises are true.
- In a deductive argument, there is a strict relation between the premises and the conclusion. The relation is strict in the sense that it is impossible for the conclusion to be false if the premises are true.
- There is something in the very pattern (or as it is called in logic, "form") of a deductive argument that ensures its validity.
- The conclusion of a deductive argument brings out what is already implicit in the premises.
- A valid deductive argument with true premises and a true conclusion is known as a sound deductive argument.

THINKING THROUGH EXERCISE 8

i. What is a deductive argument?
ii. What are the two key features of a deductive argument?
iii. What is the relation between the premises and the conclusion of a valid deductive argument?
iv. When is a deductive argument sound? Can you give an example of such an argument?

In the next chapter, we shall discuss how we can test the validity of an argument or judge if it is free from faults. But here we can say that in the case of deductive arguments, there may be two ways of determining their validity. We may try to think of an argument with the same form that has true premises but a false conclusion. We may appeal to what is known in logic as *rules of deductive reasoning* to see if any of them have been violated. This is the kind of thing we do in formal deductive logic and also in geometry and mathematics.

2.10 Inductive Arguments and Strength

Not all arguments are deductive in nature. Consider the following two arguments:

(A)	(B)
"All vegetables contain Vitamin C.	Most vegetables contain Vitamin C.
Spinach is a vegetable.	Spinach is a vegetable.
So, spinach contains Vitamin C.	So, spinach contains Vitamin C."[10]

If we look closely, we will note that there are significant differences between the two arguments, though at first glance they seem to be saying the same thing. In the case of Argument A, the first premise makes an unambiguous statement about all vegetables. Argument B does not make such a statement. And this makes all the difference. Because of this difference, in the case of Argument A, we will never find a situation wherein the premises are true but the conclusion is false. This is not so in the case of Argument B. In Argument B, it could well be the case that both the premises are true but the conclusion is false. But we must realise that the premises of Argument B make it highly possible for the conclusion to be true. In our daily lives, we draw such inferences very often.

Let us consider another example:

Most Indians are fond of cricket.
Preity Zinta is an Indian.
So, Preity Zinta is fond of cricket.

In this argument, we know that the first premise and the second premise make the conclusion more probable. Some inferences are such that the conclusion does follow from them but not with a hundred per cent certainty. In such cases, we consider the probability of the conclusion being true and also attempt to discover evidence to prove that the premises are true. This kind of argument is known as an inductive argument. *An inductive argument is an argument wherein the conclusion has a high probability of being true if the premises are true.* Sometimes we need to assess one argument against another and the best way of doing it may be by determining which of the conclusions are more probable. In induction, therefore, we judge the comparative strength of an argument by judging the probability of its conclusion.

Inductive arguments may be of many kinds. Here are the three most important kinds of inductive arguments:

i. Inductive analogy

Consider a situation wherein we have two things that are similar in many significant ways. Knowing this, we may infer that these two things are probably similar in other ways as well. For example:

I had a Sony sound system earlier on. It had a great sound box and excellent equaliser.
I just bought another Sony sound system.
So, this one will also have a great sound box and excellent equaliser.

This argument is of course not a deductive argument. And in spite of the fact that my old Sony sound system was a good one, it might well turn out that the new one that I have bought is not so good. But my past experience can be regarded as evidence that makes my conclusion more probable.

ii. Enumerative inductive generalisation

We may have come to observe a large number of things or events of a particular kind and also may have noticed that they all have one feature in common. From this observation, we may conclude that all things or events of that kind all share that feature. Let us consider an example:

All the swans I have seen in my life are white.
So, all swans are white.

This argument is of course not a deductive argument, and the appearance of a single black swan would render the conclusion false. Even still, given the premise, the probability of the conclusion being true is high.

iii. Restricted enumerative inductive generalisation

This kind of argument is very similar to the second kind of inductive argument. The only thing that makes this argument different from the previous one is that it has a conclusion that is more restricted. Let us consider an example:

All swans I have seen in my life are white.
So, most *swans are white.*

iv. Inductive argument with a singular conclusion

This kind of argument is a sort of combination of the first and third kinds of arguments. It is similar to an inductive analogy because its conclusion is a singular one. It is also similar to a restricted enumerative inductive generalisation because in this case too we are arriving at a singular conclusion from a generalisation regarding many or most cases. Let us consider an example:

KEY POINTS

Inductive arguments and strength

An inductive argument is an argument in which the conclusion has a high probability of being true given that the premises are true.

There are six kinds of inductive arguments:

i. Inductive analogy
ii. Enumerative inductive generalisation
iii. Restricted enumerative inductive generalisation
iv. Inductive argument with a singular conclusion
v. Statistical inductive argument
vi. Causal inductive argument

The strength of an inductive argument depends on the degree to which the premises make the conclusion probable.

Most children of working mothers are stubborn.
Jasmine is the child of a working mother.
So, Jasmine is stubborn.

v. Statistical inductive argument

In this kind of argument as well, we generalise based on past experiences. Here, however, there is no need for previous experiences to be uniform. What are being used in the case of such arguments are the principles of statistical regularity. "The premises describe a statistical relationship and the conclusion extrapolates that relationship from observed cases to unobserved ones."[11] Let us consider an example:

Twenty-five per cent of the students who learn the piano at the Calcutta School of Music are left-handed.
So, twenty-five per cent of all pianists are left-handed.

vi. Causal inductive argument

In this kind of argument, we conclude that an event (or an event of one kind) is the cause of another event (or another kind of event) because the premises show that both these events occur together. In other words, when we find events of one type occurring whenever events of another type occur, we conclude that there must be a causal connection between the two kinds of events. Let us consider an example:

Whenever Sunanda eats shellfish she gets rashes all over her body.
So, possibly, eating shellfish is the cause of her rashes.

We may now make some remarks about inductive arguments in general. As we can see, these arguments are very different from deductive arguments in which the conclusion follows

THINKING THROUGH EXERCISE 9

i. What is an inductive argument?
ii. Explain with the help of an example what an inductive analogy is.
iii. Explain with the help of an example what an enumerative inductive generalisation is.
iv. Explain with the help of an example what a restricted enumerative inductive generalisation is.
v. Explain with the help of an example what an inductive argument with a singular conclusion is.
vi. Explain with the help of an example what a statistical inductive argument is.
vii. Explain with the help of an example what a causal inductive argument is.
viii. What determines the strength of an argument?

from the premises with certainty and as a matter of logical necessity. The conclusion of this or any deductive argument simply spells out what is already implicit in the premises. In both these respects, an inductive argument is very different from a deductive argument. In inductive arguments, neither do conclusions follow from the premises as a matter of logical necessity and with certainty and nor does the conclusion spell out whatever is already implicit in the premises. The premises of an inductive argument simply provide evidence that *may* support the truth of the conclusion. The conclusion in a sense goes beyond the premises. So in the case of an inductive argument, we do not speak about validity, rather we speak of inductive strength. Here we are referring to the degree to which the premises make the conclusion probable.

2.11 Concluding Remarks

In this chapter, we have discussed the key notions of logic, which constitute the very essence of critical thinking. A few important points to note here are as follows:

- Critical thinking is concerned with logic.
- Critical thinking is informal logic.
- In critical thinking, we are concerned with the ability to think in ways that are supported by reason and hence critical thinking is concerned with inferences or arguments.
- In critical thinking, we discuss how one can recognise and evaluate arguments.
- An argument is presented in order to persuade a person to accept a claim that is backed by reason.
- An argument is not an opinion per se.
- An argument is not merely a description.
- An argument is a string of connected statements, some of which are premises on the basis of which one of them, i.e., the conclusion, is drawn. The premises may be regarded as a set of claims that a person puts forward in order to support a further claim that she wants to make, which is also the conclusion.
- We determine what the argument is by recognising its premises and its conclusion.
- We use certain words as premise indicators and conclusion indicators.
- There may be hidden premises in an argument.
- There may be sub-arguments and intermediate conclusions of arguments.
- We must distinguish between the truth content and the logical content of an argument.
- Validity is the key concept in a deductive argument.
- A valid argument is one in which the truth of the premises makes the truth of the conclusion certain.
- In a deductive argument, there is a strict relation between the premises and the conclusion. The relation is strict in the sense that it is impossible for the conclusion to be false if the premises are true.

- ❑ There is something in the very pattern or form of a deductive argument that ensures its validity.
- ❑ An inductive argument is one in which the conclusion has a high probability of being true if the premises are true.

2.12 More Exercises

1. Consider the following statements to check if they are supported opinions. If they are unsupported opinions, provide reasons that can support them:
   - ❑ All Bengalis support the Kolkata Knight Riders.
   - ❑ I don't believe in God because I have never seen God.
   - ❑ Smoking is bad.
   - ❑ Only tall people can be good basketball players.
   - ❑ All religious people are fanatical.
2. Consider the following sets of statements and decide which of them are arguments:
   - ❑ "Everybody who dreams is asleep. When a person is asleep, he cannot control his mind so as to to plan things. Therefore, dreams cannot be controled by a person who is dreaming."[12]
   - ❑ It is a hot summer day in Santiniketan. The students are all wearing straw hats. They have postponed their weekend picnic to avoid the heat.
   - ❑ My former boss was always telling me to change my habits and so I changed my job.
   - ❑ Since we forgot to put baking powder in the cake, the cake did not rise.
   - ❑ All boxers are short tempered. Rambo is a boxer and so he must be short tempered.
3. State the premises and the conclusions of the following arguments:
   - ❑ Ram must have loved Sita, as only a person who loves his wife can risk his and his brother's life to save her, which Ram did.
   - ❑ Since Ram was an ally of Sugriva and Bali was Sugriva's enemy, Ram considered Sugriva his enemy.
   - ❑ If all students are allowed to vote and Sujata is a student then Sujata will certainly be allowed to vote.
   - ❑ If I take up science I will get a job, and if I take up humanities I will be happy, and since I cannot take both science and humanities, I cannot both get a job and be happy.
   - ❑ "If we hit our children, they will learn that violence is acceptable, so we shouldn't physically discipline our children."[13]
4. Find the hidden premises in the following arguments:
   - ❑ I had to pay a fine because I forgot to return my library book on time.
   - ❑ The Mahabharata is still popular because it is a classic tale of the battle of good against evil.

- I cannot trust Tarun because a man who has cheated me once cannot be trusted.
- Because Russell was a logician, he couldn't be irrational.
- "If to be foolish is evil, then it is virtuous to be wise."[14]

5. Analyse the following arguments with intermediate conclusions:
   - You desire a thing only if you have had a pleasing experience with it in the past. All children desire their mother's milk. But they have not had a pleasant experience of it before this life. So they must have experienced it in some other life. Hence, rebirth exists.
   - "Your face is covered in chocolate, so it must have been you that ate my cake, so you owe me a cake."[15]
   - If it rains, the field will be wet. It has rained and the field is wet. If the field is wet, we shall not have a match and so we will not have a match.
   - All communists smoke cigars and Castro smokes cigars as he is a communist. But if you smoke cigars, you wouldn't enjoy a cigarette, and so Castro would not enjoy a cigarette.
   - "Labour is the basis of all property. From this it follows that a man owns what he makes by his own hand and the man who does not labour has no rightful property."[16]

NOTES AND REFERENCES

1. Leo Goarke, "Informal Logic", *Standford Encyclopedia of Philosophy*, http://plato.stanford.edu/entries/logic-informal, accessed on 22 April 2009.

2. Ibid.

3. T. Bowell and G. Kemp, *Critical Thinking—A Concise Guide* (London: Routledge, 2002), p. 2.

4. I am following Trudy Govier's discussion on this as we find it in her book, *A Practical Study of Argument* (Canada: Wadsworth Publishing Company, 1992)

5. Ibid., p. 6.

6. Gary Comstock, http://philosophy.tamu.edu/~gary/bioethics/reasoning/enthymemes.html, accessed on 23 April 2009.

7. Ibid.

8. Trudy Grovier, *A Practical Study of Argument*, p. 28.

9. Stan Baronett, *Logic* (Upper Saddle River, NJ: Pearson/ Prentice Hall, 2008), p. 28.

10. Ibid.

11. Trudy Govier, *A Practical Study of Argument*, p. 319.

12. Ibid., p. 11.

13. T. Bowell and G. Kemp, *Critical Thinking—A Concise Guide*, p. 37.

14. http://rhetoric.byu.edu/figures/e/enthymeme.htm, accessed on 24 April 2009.

15. http://www.criticalthinking.org.uk/unit2/fundamentals/elementsofarguments/intermediate conclusions

16. Trudy Govier, *A Practical Study of Argument*, p. 29.

3

EVALUATING ARGUMENTS: INFERENCES AND FALLACIES

Fallacious reasoning keeps us from knowing the truth, and the inability to think critically makes us vulnerable to manipulation by those skilled in the art of rhetoric.
—*Encyclopedia of Logical Fallacies*

3.1 Introduction

We have discussed in the previous chapter what an argument or inference is and how we may recognise them. We have also discussed briefly what constitutes a valid argument. We shall now discuss how we may go wrong in our arguments, that is, what causes fallacies or errors in arguments.

We must, at the outset, remember that *logical fallacies should be distinguished from factual errors*. When we make a fallacious argument, we are not necessarily factually wrong but rather we have derived an unwarranted conclusion from a set of premises that fail to give the conclusion its required logical support. We must remember that fallacious arguments are often very persuasive and in fact quite easy to come by. We must also remember that it is sometimes hard to evaluate whether an argument is fallacious. Fallacious arguments are very deftly used as rhetoric ploys in newspapers, in advertisements, in speeches made by political leaders and even by parents who want to get their children to do what they want.

Spotting a fallacious argument is especially difficult due to certain linguistic phenomena that make the fallacious argument look like a valid one. We will first talk about these linguistic phenomena that make an argument fallacious.

3.2 Linguistic Phenomena

Our language and our special use of it are primarily responsible for our difficulties in spotting fallacious arguments. Often, people use language in strange ways, which leads us astray so that spotting the mistake in an argument becomes extremely difficult. We shall be discussing the linguistic phenomena that are responsible for this.

We must realise that when we recognise or reconstruct the argument of a speaker or an author, what we are trying to do is interpret in the most accurate way what the speaker or the writer intended to convey. This interpretation is extremely important. Some linguistic phenomena work as impediments to correct interpretation. Sometimes the use of language hinders rather than facilitates this interpretation, because sometimes using language in a particular way obscures the speakers or writer's intended meaning. "So aspirant critical thinkers need to be aware of the ways in which language can work to hide writers' and speakers' meanings and must practise spotting potentially problematic sentences."[1] Let us now consider these linguistic phenomena that hinder our correct understanding.

3.2.1 Ambiguity

We may find in the course of our reconstruction of arguments presented by speakers and writers that we encounter sentences or even words that are ambiguous in the context in which they appear. Sentences or words are considered *ambiguous* when they can have more than one meaning.

Suppose I ask you to meet me at the bank. You may keep waiting for me at the river bank while I am waiting for you at the local ICICI Bank. The confusion occurred because my sentence was ambiguous due to the use of a word that could either refer to the bank of a river or the financial institution known as a bank. This kind of ambiguity is known as *lexical ambiguity*.

Not all words are ambiguous. For instance, if I were to say, "Meet me at the student canteen," you would know exactly where to meet me, unless of course there is more than one student canteen. So a term that stands for different sets of things can be regarded as ambiguous. For example, I might ask my sister to bring my phone and could not be angry if she unplugs my landline phone and gives it to me. This is because "phone" now means either mobile phone or landline phone.

Ambiguous words generate ambiguity in the sentences in which they appear. Consider this sentence:

Sushma needs a break.

This sentence could either mean:

i. Sushma needs an unexpected piece of good luck, or
ii. Sushma needs a holiday.

Consider this sentence:

Sunil asked for the light.

This sentence could either mean:

i. Sunil asked for a matchstick, or
ii. Sunil is looking for the light switch.

Consider the following sentence:

Rajiv is going to strike tomorrow.

This sentence could either mean:

i. Rajiv is going to hit someone or something tomorrow, or
ii. Rajiv is going to stop work in protest tomorrow.

We notice that the above sentences are ambiguous because an ambiguous word occurs in them. But there are also cases of sentences that are ambiguous because their structure or syntactic character could imply more than one meaning. This kind of ambiguity is known as *syntactic ambiguity*. A classic example is:

Flying planes can be dangerous.

This could either mean:

i. To fly a plane is dangerous, or
ii. Planes that are flying are dangerous.

Consider this rather funny sentence:

Kids make a wonderful snack.

This could either mean:

i. Kids can *make* snacks that are wonderful, or
ii. Kids *are* wonderful snacks.

Consider another funny sentence:

Stolen painting found by tree.

This could either have the absurd meaning:

i. A tree found a stolen painting, or
ii. A stolen painting was found next to a tree.

Consider another sentence:

The government will announce that the electricity supply is to be cut off tomorrow.

This sentence could either mean:

i. Tomorrow, the government will announce that the electricity will be cut off, or
ii. The government will announce that tomorrow the electricity will be cut off.[2]

We must realise that syntactic ambiguities are difficult to detect. In daily life, we constantly encounter sentences uttered by people or appearing in newspapers that are definitely syntactically ambiguous.

3.2.2 Vagueness

In philosophy and in mathematics, we are concerned with terms that are not ambiguous but vague. Terms whose precise meaning can never be stated are known as vague terms. They are not open to more than one interpretation and therefore they are not ambiguous. Rather, they do not have a meaning that can be precisely stated.

Suppose you have a disagreement with a friend about whether another common friend is bald or not. It would be difficult to find out which one was right because the word "bald" is a vague term. Again, suppose you ask for warm water in a restaurant and you are given a cup of water. You could find it unsatisfactory even if it is a perfectly warm cup of water. This can happen because what you mean by "warm" is vague. Consider the commonly used word, "city". What do you mean by the word "city"? We would consider both New York and New Delhi cities. But would you call Almorah or Barasat cities?

Apart from this philosophical sense of vagueness, there is another way in which a word might be vague. "The meaning of a word or expression is vague if it is indefinite or uncertain what is conveyed by the word."[3] While presenting an argument, a person might deliberately use a vague term to hide the weakness of the argument or even to cloud the judgement of the readers or listeners by evoking strong emotions. "Many highly-charged words that wield rhetorical power in public discourse are used vaguely. Examples include: 'rights', 'liberal', 'harassment', 'racism', 'sexism',"[4] as well as "secularism", "leftist", "provocative speech", etc. Let us consider the word "secular" and see how vague it is.

A person is called secular if any or many of the following characteristics may be associated with her:

- Belief in a godless system of the world
- Belief in a governmental system that has no relation to religion
- Belief in a governmental system that views all religions with equal respect
- Belief in an academic system wherein no religious training is given

- Belief in a political system that recognises politics as an autonomous sphere, one that's not subject to ecclesiastical governance, to the governance of a church or religion or the church's expression of that religion
- Anti-religion
- Atheism

Does one need to have all of these beliefs, or at least be positively disposed to all of them, in order to be called secular? We are aware that a lot of political debate has taken place with regard to what the word secular means or ought to mean in the Indian context. The absence of consensus on this issue itself demonstrates the vagueness of this term. In evaluating other people's speech, we often overlook this vagueness, but we should be very careful and make sure that we understand what the speaker intends when she uses a particular word.

3.2.3 Connotation

We often say that a word has a "double meaning". Let us consider an example of this. In Hindi, when we call a person an owl, i.e., use the word "*ullu*", we are in fact calling him an idiot and not the nocturnal bird. When we call a person an owl in English, we are calling him wise and again not the nocturnal bird.

Consider the word "chick". It usually denotes babies of chickens, but it is also a slang term used to refer to girls. The word "monkey" too refers to the animal, but we often call our children monkeys when they are naughty. So we see that a word might mean one thing, i.e., have a *primary connotation*, but it might be used to denote something else, i.e., have a *secondary connotation.*

Consider the following sentence:

One of the keys to total quality management (TQM) is involving the employees.[5]

Here, the term "key" does not mean the literal instrument used to open locks. Its usage in the sentence means, "One of the most important factors in total quality management (TQM) is involving the employees".

It is very important to understand secondary connotations while we are deciphering the meanings of sentences uttered or written by others. We need to, as we often say, read between the lines. The reason critical thinkers should take an active interest in the distinction between primary and secondary connotations is that it enables the critical thinker to get to the bottom of the speaker's and author's intention and also helps acquire rhetorical power.

3.2.4 Quantifiers

We often use words that signify quantities like how much or how many things there are or how often something happens. These are called quantifiers. Many a time, these quantifiers are not used with much precision, which might lead to mistakes in one's argument and also obscure our understanding of the speaker's and writer's intentions.

First, let us see what kinds of words are known as quantifiers. In the sentence "*All* young Indians love Hindi movies," the word "all" is the quantifier. In the sentence "*Often* we are taken in by rhetorical ploys," the word "often" is the quantifier. When we say, "*Seldom* do we find an honest politician," the word "seldom" is the quantifier. In the sentence "Lila *never* takes her car to her college," "never" is the quantifier. When we say, "*Only* the brave deserve the fair," the word "only" is the quantifier. In the sentence "*Lots* of banks now have core banking facility," the word "lots" is the quantifier.

There are many problems that we may face when we use quantifiers in an imprecise way:

- Sometimes, people use a quantifier without really intending what that particular quantifier implies. For example, even when someone says, "All young Indians love Hindi movies," it is obvious that there will be some young Indians who do not like Hindi movies. So why do we say "*All* young Indians love Hindi movies"? What we mean then is not that every single young Indian loves Hindi movies but that a very large number of young Indians love them.
- Many a time, the use of a quantifier in a sentence can be quite vague. When I say, "Some leftist politicians voted against the proposed bill," I might either mean, "Very few leftist politicians voted against the proposed bill" or "Quite a few leftist politicians voted against the proposed bill".
- Sometimes, sentences have hidden quantifiers, which make their interpretation difficult. Consider the following sentence:

  Businessmen are unscrupulous.

  At first glance, we might think that this sentence means that all businessmen are unscrupulous. But it could well mean that all the businessmen that the speaker has encountered are unscrupulous or that many businessmen are unscrupulous. By not mentioning any quantifier, the speaker hides her intentions or misleads us.
- Often, we are unable to determine the scope of a quantifier. This is a very crucial issue in formal logic but can also afflict everyday reasoning in ways that should be studied by any critical thinker. The quantifier "all" is usually used in generalisations. Let us consider an example:

  Everyone has tried drugs at some point in their lives.[6]

  This sentence will mean one thing if we restrict the use of the word "drugs" to a great extent and would mean something else entirely if we don't.

3.2.5 Opacity

Sometimes in a sentence we want to report what someone else thinks, believes, knows, intends or desires. In doing so, we need to exercise extreme caution to ensure that whatever we say about someone else's beliefs or knowledge is in consonance with what they truly believe or know. Let us take a classic example. In the famous Greek tragedy *Oedipus Rex* written by Sophocles, Oedipus tragically kills his father and marries his mother. But this he does without knowing that they were his parents. So if we say, "Oedipus desired to marry his mother," or, "Oedipus wanted to kill his own father," we would be doing a grave injustice to Oedipus. Within the context of Oedipus' desire, the term "mother" is inaptly used, giving the impression that Oedipus actually wanted to marry *his mother* knowing she was his mother, whereas the truth is he wanted to marry Jocasta whom he knew simply as Jocasta and not as his mother. Terms which occur within sentences, in which we ascribe beliefs, desires and other propositional attitudes, behave in a strange way. A term within such a sentence cannot be replaced by another term which refers to the same thing.

Many a mistake in judgement and in the evaluation of other people's arguments and speech occurs when we do not take heed of this opaque nature of words. Occurring in such contexts, these words are called opaque.

3.2.6 Rhetorical Questions

In language, we often come across questions that are asked merely for the effect that asking them produces and not in expectation of an answer. These are known as rhetorical questions. In everyday life, we often encounter such questions. When a mother asks a child, "Are you supposed to watch TV now?" she does not expect an answer but wants the child to understand that she is not supposed to watch TV at that time. Let us consider a funny conversation from the famous American cartoon, *The Simpsons*:

> Grandma Simpson and Lisa are singing Bob Dylan's "Blowin' in the Wind"—"How many roads must a man walk down/Before you call him a man?" Homer overhears them and says, "Eight!"
> Lisa: "That was a *rhetorical question*!"
> Homer: "Oh. Then, seven!"
> Lisa: "Do you even know what 'rhetorical' means?"
> Homer: "Do I know what 'rhetorical' means?"[7]

We often find such questions in newspaper articles. Suppose someone protesting against the state's intervention in the freedom of speech says, "Should my right to freedom of speech be denied because I do not agree with the ruling party's opinion on this issue?" This protestor is not asking for an answer but rather saying that though she might disagree with the opinion of the ruling party, her views should be heard as she too has freedom of speech.

A critical thinker has to recognise a rhetorical question while trying to decipher the intended meaning of a speaker or an author.

3.2.7 Irony

People often use irony to express their view. In irony, we use words to convey the opposite of their literal meaning. For instance, suppose we meet a very slow clerk at the post office and nickname him "Speedy," what we intend to imply is in fact just the opposite of what the word "speedy" means.

We make ironical statements about the weather all the time. Suppose Aban comes home sweating and says, "Oh! It's freezing outside!" what he means is that it is extremely hot outside. Suppose Arka says to his brother who is annoying him, "I am very pleased with you!" what he means is that he is annoyed with his brother. Mark Twain once said, "Get your facts first, then you can distort them as you please". This is another good example of irony.

KEY POINTS

Fallacies and linguistic phenomena

- ❑ Our language and our special use of the language are primarily responsible for our difficulties in spotting fallacious arguments.
- ❑ Phenomena responsible for difficulties in spotting fallacies in arguments are:
  - i. Ambiguity
  - ii. Vagueness
  - iii. Connotation
  - iv. Quantifiers
  - v. Opacity
  - vi. Rhetorical questions
  - vii. Irony

THINKING THROUGH EXERCISE 1

- i. Why do we have problems in spotting fallacies in an argument?
- ii. When is the use of language ambiguous? How does it affect an argument?
- iii. What is vagueness? How does it affect an argument?
- iv. What is connotation? How do we distinguish between primary and secondary connotation?
- v. What are quantifiers? What are the problems that we face if quantifiers are not used properly?
- vi. When is the context of the occurrence of a word opaque?
- vii. What is a rhetorical question?
- viii. What is irony?

A critical thinker should be able to recognise and consider the possibility of irony in the words of a speaker and an author.

3.3 FALLACIES

We have earlier discussed that inferences are offered in order to support the claim that is made in the conclusion. When an inference does not manage to provide adequate logical support, a fallacy is committed and the argument is rendered invalid. The concept of validity and the issue of fallacies may be addressed either formally or informally. In formal logic, we are concerned with logical errors in the structure or the form of an argument, and so these fallacies are *formal fallacies*. The reason these are called formal fallacies is that there is something in the very form of the arguments in question that makes the arguments turn out to be fallacious. *Informal fallacies* however are not fallacies generated due to any peculiarity in the form of the argument. There may be linguistic reasons pertaining to the phenomena just discussed that lead to these fallacies. Broadly, we may divide informal fallacies into the following kinds: (1) the fallacy of ambiguity, (2) the fallacy of unwarranted assumption and (3) the fallacy of relevance.

3.3.1 The Fallacy of Ambiguity

We have already discussed how language can be ambiguous and lead to difficulties in the interpretation of a speaker's or author's intention. We shall now discuss in detail the fallacies that result due to ambiguities in language.

i. Equivocation

When a word is used equivocally, there is always a chance of misunderstandings and fallacious reasoning. If however a word is used in two senses then there is a fallacy of equivocation. Consider this argument:

> *He's a real pain the neck.*
> *Cortisone shots help relieve neck pain.*
> *Maybe a good dose of cortisone will change his attitude.*[8]

In the first premise, the expression "pain in the neck" is used to imply that the person being spoken of is irritating in nature. The same expression in the second premise is used to refer to a discomfort in the neck. In politics, rather in political debates, words are often used equivocally. For instance, in USA, all presidential campaigns focus on the issue of unemployment. During these debates, the contending parties' speeches often refer to different meanings of the term "unemployed" from *persons who are not employed at all* to meaning *persons who are collecting unemployment benefits*. In Indian politics, a lot of rhetoric on the concept of secularism thrives on the equivocal use of the word "secular"—sometimes used to mean *having nothing to do with religion* and sometimes used to mean *respect for all religions*. A critical thinker should trace words that might be used equivocally within a discourse and be clear as to what is being meant by the word in a specific situation.

ii. Amphiboly

While fallacy of equivocation results from lexical ambiguity, fallacy of amphiboly results from syntactic ambiguity. We may land up making mistakes in interpretation if a speaker or writer uses statements that are grammatically or syntactically unclear. Consider the following sentences:

- *Mother saw Chetna walking by.*
- *He was shot in the train in the back in the sleeping car.*[9]
- *US President Bush has cancelled a trip to Scotland to play golf.*[10]

The first sentence could mean either that mother was walking by and saw Chetna while doing so, or that mother saw Chetna who was walking by. Consider the second sentence. It could either mean that the man was shot in his back while he was in the sleeping car of a train or that he was shot when he was at the back of the train's sleeping car. The third sentence could either mean that the US president cancelled his Scotland trip so that he could play golf or that he cancelled his Scotland trip on which he was supposed to play golf. A critical thinker should spot such syntactic ambiguities or "amphibolies" and enquire into what exactly his interlocutor means.

iii. Composition

Often, people make the mistake of attributing the property of the constituent parts of a whole to the whole itself. This leads to a fallacy of composition. Suppose we have the following argument:

> *None of the children in this group can make a terrible noise.*
> *Therefore, together they will not be able to make a terrible noise.*

It is not difficult to spot the problem with this argument. Although individually the children may not be able to make noise, they may well be capable of making a lot of noise collectively. There can be many examples of arguments committing such a fallacy of composition. Below are some more examples:

- *The thread you are using is easily torn, so the garment you are making will be easily torn.*[11]
- *Each piece I use to make this collage is square and so the collage too will be square.*
- *Our cells are tiny and so we are also tiny because we are made up of cells.*

We must now carefully notice the first argument. It definitely involves a fallacy because the threads may well be easily torn and yet the cloth may be sturdy. But consider a minor change in the argument:

> *The thread you are using is blue. So the garment you make out of it will also be blue.*

Notice here that the colour of the constituent threads gives the colour to the whole garment. So this argument is not fallacious. Thus, sometimes, an inference regarding the property of the whole made on the basis of the properties of its parts is not wrong. A critical thinker should be able to recognise when a composition turns out to be fallacious and when not.

iv. Division

Just as we sometimes mistakenly attribute the properties of the parts to the whole, we can also attribute properties of the whole to its parts. This is also a mistake. If we think that because a man is large, the cells that make up his body are also large, then we are obviously making a mistake. Consider the following argument:

> *The Conservative Party won in the French election.*
> *Therefore, each and every Frenchman is a conservative.*

It would be wrong to think that in this argument the premise really supports the conclusion. A critical thinker should never offer or defend such arguments.

v. Emphasis

Sometimes people twist words and emphasise things that are not originally emphasised upon for their own benefit. In this way, what one does is subtly distort another's speech and shift the emphasis for one's own benefit. Fallacy of emphasis occurs when incorrect emphasis is placed on words composing the premise of an argument so as to arrive at the desired conclusion. This results in a distortion of the argument itself. Below is an example:

> *Mother: You spilled the coffee on the carpet.*
> *Jasmine: I spilled the coffee?*
> *Mother: There you are. You admit it.*

Notice here that Jasmine's mother discounts the note of interrogation in Jasmine's utterance, considers it as a statement and then uses it against Jasmine to substantiate her accusation.

Here is another example. Take a case where one says: "Adam thinks it will work." While speaking, emphasis could be on the word "think", making it sound like:

> "Adam *thinks* it will work."

This utterance changes the meaning altogether. This emphasis will make the sentence mean that Adam just has an unsupported hunch.

vi. Straw man fallacy

Often, in a debate, a contending party constructs the opponent's stand in a very weak way so that it is easy to refute it. If we do this then we are committing the straw man fallacy. Let us consider an interesting example:

> Cardinal William Levada, head of the Vatican's Congregation for the Doctrine of the Faith, claims that Richard Dawkins and others have argued that evolution proves there is no God. It does not require much of an argument to show that that notion is absurd, which is the cardinal's position. However, neither Dawkins nor any other atheist I'm aware of has ever held such a position. The cardinal is refuting an argument nobody holds. Dawkins's position is that evolution makes atheism intellectually respectable or something to that effect. That is, evolution fits nicely into a naturalistic worldview. We're all aware, atheists and theists alike, that there have been logically coherent metaphysical views that incorporate both the supernatural and evolution of species. Many atheists would argue that there is no need for an appeal to the supernatural in order to explain the existence of the universe or the evolution of species on our planet. God is an unnecessary hypothesis. Being unnecessary doesn't make it false.[12]

Notice here that it is wrong to assume that your opponent has a weak argument. It would be wrong to assume that atheists like Dawkins are saying that the theory of evolution proves that God does not exist. Certainly no theory of evolution can prove that or will ever aim to prove such a thing. All that they prove is that we can explain life on earth in a naturalistic way and in that case we do not need to assume the existence of a conscious Divine Creator. Not all theistic arguments are of the straw man variety simply because they acknowledge the point that the atheists are really making. The line of argument that they take is that it is indeed necessary to acknowledge the existence of God to explain life on earth and this explanation is a better one than the naturalistic one.

vii. Red herring fallacy

A red herring fallacy is actually an extreme sort of fallacy of emphasis. When someone presents an argument that actually introduces a topic that is completely irrelevant to the topic under consideration just to divert attention from the original issue, one is committing a red herring fallacy. For instance, suppose we are discussing whether the admission criteria for undergraduate courses in universities and colleges should be made stricter. Someone might argue the following:

> *I think we ought to make the selection criteria stricter because after all we are in a period of recession and we don't want to lose our jobs.*

Notice that neither the possibility of losing jobs nor the recession has anything to do with the criteria that should be used to select people fit for undergraduate courses. Below is another example of a red herring fallacy:

> *Evolution is impossible because the Big Bang is a totally unacceptable theory because it defies the word of our loving Creator, He who sent His only Son, our Lord.*[13]

Here too the argument is diverting our attention from evolution to the Big Bang Theory, which is quite tangential to the discussion of evolution.

3.3.2 The Fallacy of Unwarranted Assumption

An argument suffers from the fallacy of unwarranted assumption when it either contains a premise that is poorly based or a conclusion that is inadequately supported. We are able to demonstrate that such an argument is fallacious when we can expose the premise that lacks support.

i. Begging the question

An argument "begs the question" if the conclusion that it intends to prove is already assumed in its premises. Suppose I say the following:

> *Tobacco chewing is a cause of oral cancer because there is a causal relation between tobacco and cancer.*

We see that the conclusion, which wants to establish the fact that tobacco chewing is the cause of oral cancer, assumes the premise that there is a cause-effect relation between tobacco and cancer.

Consider another example:

God's word is always true, the Bible is God's word, and the Bible says God exists. So God exists.[14]

Notice here that if we want to establish that God exists then we cannot do so by appealing to the Bible, which is assumed to be the word of God.

ii. Complex question

A complex question fallacy occurs when we ask a question that makes a hidden assumption that is unwarranted. For example, a lawyer asks a witness, "So have you stopped lying?" This makes the unwarranted assumption that the witness used to lie. This is called a complex question because here we are actually asking two questions: 1. Do you usually lie? 2. Have you stopped doing so now? We are assuming that the answer to the first question is "Yes" and then asking the second question right away without really asking the first. This makes the question a complex one with a hidden unwarranted assumption.

Consider another example:

So, are the left parties now regretting their highhandedness?

There are really two questions here:

- ❑ Do the left parties acknowledge that they have been high handed?
- ❑ Do the left parties regret their high handedness?

And the complex question has been asked with the assumption that the answer to the first question is "Yes".

iii. Hasty generalisation

If one makes a generalisation based on only a few instances then the generalisation would be hasty. Let us consider a humorous example:

Someone sneezed when I went out today. I missed my interview. So whenever someone sneezes when we are going to do some important work, we will fail at doing that work properly.

Though this seems funny, this is the kind of generalisation we make all the time. Consider another example:

The only two Italians I ever knew belonged to the Mafia. So if you ask me, all Italians are crooks.[15]

Here is yet another example:

Jason sings in a band and he takes drugs. So all who sing in a band are drug addicts.

A critical thinker should avoid these kinds of generalisations at any cost.

iv. Biased sample

If while making a general statement we only choose samples that are sure to conform to the general thesis of what we want to prove then the sample is biased.

A study conducted in Bengal and Assam shows 85 per cent of the people love to eat fish. So 85 per cent of Indians love fish.

This argument suffers from the fallacy of a biased sample because Bengalis and Assamese people are primarily fish eaters but that is not the case with the entire population of India. So just by studying the food habits of Bengalis and Assamese we cannot make a generalisation about all Indians.

Consider another example:

An opinion poll conducted in Mumbai colleges showed that 90 per cent of the students watch, on average, one Hindi film every month. So all Indian students watch one Hindi film every month, on average.

It is clear from this argument that the survey was conducted just on students from Mumbai who are more likely to watch Hindi films than those in any other part of the country. So this statement also suffers from the fallacy of a biased sample.

v. Unqualified generalisation (dicto simpliciter)

Sometimes when we make a generalisation, we do not qualify it to exclude the exceptions. This amounts to a fallacy of unqualified generalisation. For instance, suppose someone says the following:

No one should spend money on psychiatrists.

Of course this does not take into account the fact that people who are suffering from psychological problems may need to pay a psychiatrist for treatment.

Consider another example:

Every religious Hindu ought to fast on Thursdays.

Of course, anyone who believes in this practice would not want that infants and ailing people should do the same.

Here is another example:

Everyone should exercise to keep fit.

This would not apply to those who are barred from doing physical exercise due to orthopaedic problems.

vi. False cause

In an argument if we assume one thing to be the cause of another, though there are reasons to consider other causes, then we commit the fallacy of false cause. For example:

Srinath lost his job because he forgot to fast on Tuesday last week.

Obviously, there might be better reasons for Srinath losing his job. For instance, there could be a recession or Srinath might not have been working properly.

I quote from Stan Baronett's *Logic* here to show how often we may go wrong in assuming one thing to be the cause of another when there are far better candidates. The example is especially relevant in the Indian context.

Consider the following inference:

> "I told you not to trust him. After all, he was born under the sign of Aquarius in the year of the Rabbit. He can't help himself, the stars dictate his behaviour."
>
> Astrology places human behaviour under the influence of the planets and stars. It claims that we are causally connected to astral influences that occurred at the time of our birth and continue throughout our lives. Of course these causal claims do not have any credible scientific evidence in their support; they are based mostly on anecdotal evidence. In addition, the general personality traits associated with astrology can be applied to anyone.[16]

Moreover, if we make a thorough enquiry, we will find some credible causes for the behaviour of the person in question.

vii. Coincidence

When we take a coincidental connection between two events as indicative of a strict causal relation then we commit the fallacy of coincidence. Suppose I say that an astrologer predicted that I would get a job when I am twenty-five and I do in fact get a job at the age of twenty-five. I could then conclude that I will also get married when I am twenty-nine because the astrologer said so too. Such an argument would be committing the fallacy of coincidence because it is purely due to chance that one of the predictions of the astrologer came true. It does not guarantee that all his predictions are bound to be true.

viii. Post hoc fallacy

Post hoc or *post hoc ergo propter hoc* (after this, therefore, because of this) is a fallacious argument in which we consider an event x as the cause of an event y simply because x has occurred before y. Suppose I forget to fast on a Tuesday, fall ill after three weeks and assume I fell ill because I did not fast. This is an argument that commits the fallacy of *post hoc ergo propter hoc*. Another example of such an argument is deciding not to have a bath before exams because you performed exceptionally well on an exam one day when you did not have time for a bath. What will most probably happen is that you will not do well in the exam and also just end up being dirty.

ix. Common cause fallacy

Sometimes we assume an event x to be the cause of an event y whereas in reality both x and y have been caused by z. In such a case, we commit the fallacy of common cause. For instance, suppose my child has a high temperature and then develops rashes and I conclude that the temperature is the cause of the rashes. Here, I do not realise that my child actually has a temperature and the rashes both because of a viral infection. So the high temperature is not the cause of the rashes.

x. Slippery slope

Suppose I argue that an event *y* must inevitably follow from an event *x*. My argument will be a good one if I have enough justification to support this *inevitability*. However, without any good justification, I shall be adopting an argument that commits the slippery slope fallacy.

Suppose I say the following:

> *We've got to stop them from banning pornography. Once they start banning one form of literature, they will never stop. Next thing you know, they will be burning all the books!*[17]

I will be committing the fallacy of slippery slope as I am not in a position to show that burning books is a behaviour that will inevitably follow from the act of banning pornographic literature.

xi. Gambler's fallacy

This fallacy gets its name from the gambler's instinctive belief that if she has lost many times in the recent past then the next time she gambles she will win. What the gambler does is to assume that "the repeated occurrence of an event that departs from the expected norm indicates that the event will cease soon".[18]

Consider an example:

> *Jane: I'll be able to buy that car I always wanted soon.*
> *Bill: Why, did you get a raise?*
> *Jane: No. But you know how I've been playing the lottery all these years?*
> *Bill: Yes, you buy a ticket for every drawing, without fail.*
> *Jane: And I've lost every time.*
> *Bill: So why do you think you will win this time?*
> *Jane: Well, after all those losses I'm due for a win.*[19]

What is wrong in this line of argument is that there is no guarantee of luck.

xii. False dichotomy

When in an argument we do not mention all the alternatives there are to choose from but mention only some, we commit the fallacy of false dichotomy or false dilemma. Suppose we want to know where a friend of ours could be and we say:

> *Anushka is either at college or at home. We called her home and she is not there, so she is at college.*

This argument seems valid but it has a false dichotomy as its premise. Anushka could in fact be in a third place apart from college and her home. She could have gone to the cinema or the library or for a walk or to the coffee house. We are not taking into consideration all the alternative places she could be and so our argument suffers from the fallacy of false dichotomy.

3.3.3 The Fallacy of Relevance

Critical thinkers have to be careful about whether the relevant details are being considered in an argument. Irrelevance is a flaw that no critical thinker can afford to ignore. The fallacy of relevance occurs when we fail to provide adequate reasons for believing in the conclusions we wish to derive. People might make convincing attempts to persuade others through illogical means. Many of the fallacies of relevance were identified by medieval and renaissance logicians and so many of them have Latin names.

i. Appeal to inappropriate authority (argumentum ad verecundiam)

Suppose I say, "Isaac Newton believed in astrology, so there must be something to it". Now it is true that Newton was a wise man and he was an authority on physics, but to consider him an authority on other things would be wrong. We often appeal to this sort of inappropriate authority. Suppose I say, "I must have fractured my fifth meta-tarsal because my grandmother says so and she knows everything". The obvious question that you should ask is, "Is your grandmother an orthopaedist?" If my grandmother is not an orthopaedist then there is no reason for me to take her word as authoritative. Suppose your philosophy teacher says to you, "The spider is an insect" and you argue with your friends citing your teacher as a credible authority, you would be wrong in doing so. You need to ask a biologist or entomologist and you will come to know that spiders are not insects but belong to a large group of animals called arthropoda. We must, as critical thinkers, be able to spot who is and who isn't an expert in the matter we are discussing and accordingly take their word as authoritative.

ii. Ad hominem

Ad hominem is the exact opposite of the fallacy of inappropriate authority. When we are judging the veracity of a person's words, if we are biased and if we say that their words cannot be true because they have some sort of character flaw, then we would be committing the ad hominem fallacy. For instance, suppose I say, "Rakesh cannot be right when he says that spiders are not insects because he once cheated while he was playing chess with me". Rakesh could well have cheated on a game of chess and yet be an expert on spiders.

Suppose someone says, "Why should we accept what Max Müller said about Indian philosophy, he was not even Indian". This would be totally inappropriate because there is absolutely no reason to think that only Indians can be experts in Indian philosophy.

iii. Tu quoque

Tu quoque may also be called the "look who's talking" fallacy. Suppose your father who has been a smoker all his life tells you, "Don't smoke because smoking is bad for your health". If your response to this is to say, "Look who's talking" and you continue smoking, then you would be committing the fallacy of tu quoque. You may feel that a smoker cannot have the right to give advice to others about smoking, but what he says might nonetheless be true. So by retorting, "Look who's talking," you cannot get away from the wrong you are doing.

Suppose Political Party X, which is well known for rigging elections, complains that Political Party Y is rigging an election and Party Y retorts, "Look who's talking". Do Party X's misdeeds make Party Y's act permissible or laudable? This demonstrates how wrong this way of arguing is.

iv. Non sequitur

"Non sequitur" means "does not follow" in Latin. When the conclusion does not follow from the premise, it is the fallacy of non sequitur. In a sense, all the formal fallacies are cases of non sequitur. When we speak of the informal non sequitur fallacy, we are speaking of arguments wherein an unsupported or inadequately supported opinion is presented as a valid conclusion.

Suppose I have an ailment and I have tried all kinds of medical treatments that have failed and I then decide to try faith healing. This is an example of non sequitur reasoning because the failure of all medical treatments does not ensure the success of faith healing.

Consider another example:

I hear the rain falling outside my window; therefore, the sun is not shining.[20]

Since it can rain even when the sun is shining, the premises do not support the conclusion. This is a classic case of non sequitur.

v. Divine fallacy

The divine fallacy is a kind of non sequitur but it warrants a special mention. It often happens that when we cannot explain a phenomenon, we resort to thinking that God must be responsible for it. For example, when people did not know the cause of thunder and lightning, they thought it was an expression of God's rage.

vi. Appeal to emotion (argumentum ad populum)

Suppose an advertisement for diamond jewellery says, "If you do not give your wife a diamond ring for your wedding, you don't love her". This advertisement is appealing to your emotional weakness to get you to buy the diamond ring. Of course, buying someone a diamond ring is not a prerequisite for loving that person. As the age-old saying goes, "Money can't buy me love!"

We encounter this sort of thinking or argument very often in everyday life. For instance, it can be seen in a mother's refrain, "Eat another chapatti otherwise I will be very angry".

Consider another case: Ajay wants to marry the girl he loves. His mother is dead against it. She says, "Marry the girl of my choice and you will make me very happy. If you don't, I will be sad forever". All these forms of persuasion make unwarranted appeals to the emotion.

vii. Appeal to pity (argumentum ad misericordiam)

If while persuading someone we appeal to his or her sense of pity then we would be committing the fallacy of appeal to pity. Suppose an applicant for a job who gives a bad interview says to the interviewers,

"I am the poorest and the most needy of all the applicants and if I don't get this job my entire family will starve to death and so you ought to give me this job."

As in the previous case, this is a kind of reasoning we often encounter. It makes us feel awkward and may make us take wrong judgements. A critical thinker should learn to differentiate between emotions and thoughts backed by reason.

viii. Appeal to force (argumentum ad baculum)

Appeal to force is possibly the opposite of appeal to pity. Suppose in an interview the candidate says to the interviewers,

"You better give me this job or else you will get into trouble because I am the son of the local MLA."

Here the candidate is trying to force the experts to accept what he wants them to.

Consider another example:

A teacher says to her students: "If you do not help me with my work then you will get low marks in the exam."

Here too the teacher is resorting to force to get her students to do what she wants.

ix. Inference from ignorance (argumentum ad ignoratiam)

This kind of argument either says something is true because it cannot be proved to be false or declares something false because it cannot be proved to be true. Two classic cases of such an argument are:

- God must exist because I cannot prove that He doesn't exist.
- God does not exist because I cannot prove that He does.

Our ignorance about arguments proving or disproving God's existence cannot be a good reason for thinking either that God does or does not exist. This line of reasoning commits the fallacy of inference from ignorance.

x. Appeal to tradition

Often, we are asked to follow a course of action because it is in keeping with traditional norms. This is usually not a good reason for following that course of action at all. For instance, there was a time when it was customary for men to have more than one wife. If today someone marries more than one woman and appeals to tradition then that would not be correct. Let us consider another example:

When Thomas Alva Edison invented the electric light bulb, one could have said, "You can't possibly expect your new electric light to replace tried and true gaslight, Mr Edison."[21]

This would be entirely wrong. It does not follow from the fact the gaslight is time-tested that no other technology would ever be able to replace it.

KEY POINTS

Fallacies

- Fallacies may be formal or informal.
- Informal fallacies are of three kinds:
  - i. Fallacy of ambiguity
  - ii. Fallacy of unwarranted assumption
  - iii. Fallacy of relevance
- Fallacies of ambiguity can be of the following kinds:
  - i. Equivocation
  - ii. Amphiboly
  - iii. Composition
  - iv. Division
  - v. Emphasis
  - vi. Straw man fallacy
  - vii. Red herring fallacy
- Fallacies of unwarranted assumption can be of the following kinds:
  - i. Begging the question
  - ii. Complex question
  - iii. Hasty generalisation
  - iv. Biased sample
  - v. Unqualified generalisation
  - vi. False cause
  - vii. Coincidence
  - viii. Post hoc fallacy
  - ix. Common cause fallacy
  - x. Slippery slope
  - xi. Gambler's fallacy
  - xii. False dichotomy
- Fallacies of relevance may be of the following kinds:
  - i. Appeal to inappropriate authority (*argumentum ad verecundiam)*
  - ii. Ad hominem
  - iii. Tu quoque
  - iv. Non sequitur
  - v. Divine fallacy
  - vi. Appeal to emotion (*argumentum ad populum)*
  - vii. Appeal to pity (*argumentum ad misericordiam)*
  - viii. Appeal to force (*argumentum ad baculum)*
  - ix. Inference from ignorance (*argumentum ad ignoratiam)*
  - x. Appeal to tradition
  - xi. Irrelevant conclusion (*ignoratio elenchi)*

THINKING THROUGH EXERCISE 2

i. What are the differences between a formal fallacy and an informal fallacy?
ii. What do we mean by the fallacy of ambiguity?
iii. What do we mean by the fallacy of unwarranted assumption?
iv. What do we mean by the fallacy of relevance?
v. Explain all the fallacies of ambiguity.
vi. Explain all the fallacies of unwarranted assumption.
vii. Explain all the fallacies of relevance.

xi. Irrelevant conclusion (ignoratio elenchi)

Sometimes in presenting an argument we provide evidence that is not exactly relevant to the conclusion we wish to arrive at. We have a fine example to illustrate this:

All children should get ample attention from their parents.
Parents who work full time cannot give ample attention to their children.
Therefore, mothers should not work full time.

This is an argument we often hear. Notice here that the premises do not support the conclusion at hand. It rather supports the conclusion, "All parents (and not just mothers) should not work full time". Instead, the argument only refers to the woman's responsibility to raise her children, keeping the men's responsibility towards their children out of the picture altogether.

3.4 The Relevance of Relevance

Of all the things we have so far said about arguments, what is most important is that the evidence that we cite in an argument must be relevant in such a way that it really supports the purported conclusion. We are now going to discuss the requirement of relevance once more, as it is extremely important for a critical thinker.

When a critical thinker assesses his own thought process or the thought process of another, what she does is create a reconstruction of the key arguments presented. One of the things that she needs to do is to eliminate all the extraneous aspects from the argument and retain only that which can be considered as truly relevant to the argument. Suppose our argument is as follows:

We can't go to Delhi on Diwali because we shall not get a train ticket. Diwali is the festival of light. People distribute sweets among their friends and relatives during Diwali. We can't go to Delhi on Diwali because we have not booked tickets ahead of time and we shall not get a train ticket.

In this argument, the conclusion is "We can't go to Delhi on Diwali because we shall not get a train ticket". That Diwali is a festival of lights and that people distribute sweets during Diwali is irrelevant to the conclusion. However, the fact that it is usually difficult to get a train ticket during Diwali if you have not booked well ahead of time is relevant to it. A critical thinker must first reconstruct the argument by sifting out that which is relevant and eliminating what is irrelevant. So, to a critical thinker, the argument will look like this:

We can't go to Delhi on Diwali because we have not booked tickets ahead of time and we shall not get a train ticket. So we can't go to Delhi on Diwali, because we shall not get a train ticket.

There are two ways in which a piece of information may be relevant to the conclusion: (1.) positive relevance and (2.) negative relevance. If the information is neither positively nor negatively relevant then the information is just irrelevant. Let us try to define these three concepts:

Suppose we have an argument of the following form:

$$\frac{X}{\text{Therefore } Y}$$

i. X is *positively relevant* to Y if and only if the truth of X would count in favour of the truth of Y.
ii. X is *negatively relevant* to Y if and only if the truth of X would count against the truth of Y.
iii. X is *irrelevant* to Y if and only if the truth of X would neither count for nor against the truth of Y.

Let us illustrate these three concepts:

i. Example of positive relevance:

Basketball is a game in which height is a great advantage.
Therefore, basketball is a game for which physical characteristics of players make a substantial difference in people's ability. [22]

Notice here that the truth of the premise would count as evidence towards the truth of the conclusion.

ii. Example of negative relevance

Eating too many nuts may increase the cholesterol level.
Therefore, eating nuts is a healthy habit.

Notice that the truth of the premise would count as a piece of evidence against the conclusion.

iii. Example of irrelevance

Tania is rich and a snob.
Therefore, she cannot be good at art history.

Notice that the truth of the premise neither counts as evidence in favour of the conclusion nor as evidence against it.

As is clear from our discussion, only when a premise is positively relevant to the conclusion is it able to prove the conclusion. It would be good to mention here the different ways in which a premise or a set of premises may be regarded as positively relevant. In the second chapter, we have discussed deductive and inductive arguments. When a premise is positively relevant in the case of a deductive argument, its relevance is of a special kind, very different from the kind of relevance that a positively relevant premise of an inductive argument.

In a valid deductive argument, the premises provide entailing evidence. As we have already explained in the second chapter, a piece of evidence is entailing if it is impossible that the evidential sentences are true but the conclusion is false. In a deductive argument, the premises are relevant to the conclusion in the sense that the conclusion is already contained within the premises themselves. All that the argument does is bring out the conclusion, which is already within the premises. So, in this sense, the premises are *completely relevant* to the conclusion in the case of a deductive argument.

Let us consider the nature of relevance in the case of inductive reasoning. In inductive reasoning, we extrapolate from past events to future. In this kind of induction, the entire burden of relevance rests upon the assumption that regularities that we have experienced in the past will continue to hold in the future. On the basis of this assumption, past events become relevant to future events. The same will happen when we argue from observed regularities to unobserved regularities.

KEY POINTS

The relevance of relevance:

- ❑ Of all the things we have said about arguments, what is most important is that the evidence that we cite in an argument must be relevant.
- ❑ When we make a claim Y on the basis of X, X can be:
    - i. Positively relevant to Y
    - ii. Negatively relevant to Y
    - iii. Irrelevant to Y
- ❑ The notion of evidence when applied to deductive reasoning is different from the notion of evidence when applied to inductive reasoning.
- ❑ An argument is acceptable if the premises provide sufficient evidence for the conclusion.

THINKING THROUGH EXERCISE 3

i. Why is relevance so important for an argument?
ii. What do we mean by positive relevance?
iii. What do we mean by negative relevance?
iv. When is a sentence irrelevant for another sentence?
v. How is the concept of relevance when applied in the case of deduction different from the concept of relevance when applied in the case of induction?
vi. Why should the premises be sufficient for the conclusion in order for the argument to be acceptable?

In all other cases of informal fallacies, the premises provide us with reasons to believe in the conclusion. Fallacies occur whenever it does not seem reasonable to accept the evidence at hand as supporting the conclusion.

3.5 Sufficiency

When we evaluate an argument, we question whether the premises are sufficient for establishing the conclusion. In the case of a valid deductive argument, it is obvious that the premises are sufficient because the conclusion is culled from the premises. But in the case of inductive reasoning, this question of sufficiency becomes extremely important.

In inductive arguments, the kind of evidence we offer consists of facts that we cite or statistical data that we think is relevant to the conclusion. We also refer to past experience, make comparisons or give examples to substantiate our claim. For each kind of evidence we present, we must first question whether it is sufficient to establish the conclusion or not.

Relevance and sufficiency together lead to premises that are able to support the conclusion. All these we have to remember are properties of the evidence we offer for our conclusion. So an evaluation of relevance and sufficiency would count as an evaluation of evidence in general.

3.6 Concluding Remarks

In this chapter, we have discussed the linguistic phenomena responsible for our inability in spotting flaws in arguments. We have also discussed the different kinds of informal fallacies that might result from our inability to cope with these phenomena. We must remember that we should ask ourselves the following questions when we are evaluating an argument:

i. Is this an argument?
ii. Is this a persuasive argument in which reasons are given for the conclusion?
iii. Are the reasons acceptable?
iv. Is the evidence provided by the premises in support of the conclusion relevant?

v. Is the evidence provided by the premises in support of the conclusion sufficient?
vi. Are the generalisations made (if any) hasty or unqualified?
vii. Are the samples we have considered free from bias?
viii. Are the examples representative of the case at hand?
ix. Has enough background information been provided by the argument so that we can assess the reasons and the evidence provided in the argument?
x. Are there any counter-examples?
xi. Is the argument strong enough to refute objections?

A critical thinker has to be on a constant vigil.

3.7 More Exercises

1. Each of the following passages contains a fallacy of ambiguity. Determine the fallacy that best fits each case and explain your answer:

   - ❑ You called Mr B the Big Boss but he is only five feet tall!
   - ❑ Each brick that has gone into the making of this building is small so the building is also small.
   - ❑ Mother: You will finish your homework before you watch TV.
   - ❑ Sejal: I will?
   - ❑ Mother: I'm glad you agree to finish your homework.
   - ❑ Aishwarya is very beautiful. Her spleen must also be very beautiful.
   - ❑ Just waiting to be assaulted, the thug saw the woman standing alone on the desolate street.
   - ❑ My mother wants me to take piano lessons because studies show that early music training helps students in math. But pianos cost a lot of money and even if we could afford one our apartment is too small to occupy a full-size piano.
   - ❑ Chetan was caught chatting with his friends on the computer when he was supposed to be working on the project. The boss will soon fire anyone who is caught going to the toilet or taking a coffee break.
   - ❑ Gazing from the balcony, the floating clouds touched Mira's heart.
   - ❑ Rustam used the best paints available so his painting will also be the best.
   - ❑ I hear that there will be some heated debates in the meeting today. We ought to turn the air conditioner on.

2. Each of the following passages contains a fallacy of unwarranted assumption. Determine the fallacy that best fits each case and explain your answer:

   - ❑ That thief can never speak truthfully because whenever he opens his mouth he starts making up stories.

- Have you stopped copying from others these days?
- I have met three Bengalis and they all sing Rabindrasangeet. There must be something about this weather that makes all Bengalis sing Rabindrasangeet.
- All young Italian students listen to the Italian Premier Football League commentary on the radio on Sunday afternoons. So all Italians are fond of football.
- Exercise is good for health, so everyone ought to exercise.
- Jagdeep brought his accident upon himself by continuing to drive along the street even after a black cat crossed his path.
- I had a bad dream about my pet dog and now it has been hit by a car.
- For three consecutive weeks, whenever I have starched my clothes and put them out in the sun, it has started to rain. It has been very hot and dry for five days. We could do with some rain. I know what to do: I'll just starch my clothes and put them out in the sun.
- Ritu has been coughing and now she has a runny nose. The runny nose must have been caused by the cough.
- Now you want women to have equal rights, next you will want men and women to share the same toilet.
- Everyone who is not with the political leader is against the political leader.
- I have missed the school bus nineteen times. This time I will get it.

3. Each of the following passages contains a fallacy of relevance. Determine the fallacy that best fits each case and explain your answer:

   - My music teacher says it will rain next week, so it will rain next week.
   - I can't take any advice from my grandmother. She is 92 and all her ideas are old fashioned.
   - I won't listen to you if you ask me to drive carefully, because you get fined every other day for rash driving.
   - If women should have equal rights then the women in our class should be allowed to shave their beards.
   - I don't know how a peacock has such a beautiful tail. God must have designed it.
   - If you don't take me to Goa for a holiday I will know you don't love me.
   - Last year I broke my wrist and then had a back injury, so you must give me this desk job.
   - If you don't come to my class then I will ask all the other teachers to give you low grades.
   - Nobody has been able to prove that there is no life on Mars; therefore, there is life on Mars.
   - You must wear a saree for your wedding because your mother and grandmother did so too.

- ❑ Professor Suri is very strict about marking. He also wants his students to attend all the classes, do all the necessary practice at home and also expects them to do library work and gather research material. Therefore, he does not want his students to be happy.
- ❑ I haven't yet looked in my office for the book that I cannot find. So it must be in the office.

NOTES AND REFERENCES

1. Tracy Bowell and Gary Kemp, *Critical Thinking—A Concise Guide* (London: Routledge, 2002), p. 20.

2. Ibid., p. 21.

3. Ibid., p. 24.

4. Ibid.

5. http://eca.state.gov/forum/vols/vol39/no2/p2.htm, accessed on 6 April 2009.

6. Ibid., p. 32.

7. "Mother Simpson," *The Simpsons*, Fox Broadcasting Company, 19 November 1995. Taken from http://grammar.about.com/b/2010/02/12/do-you-have-any-rhetorical-questions.htm (Author: Richard Nordquist), accessed on 14 April 2009.

8. Stan Baronett, *Logic* (Upper Saddle River, NJ: Pearson-Prentice Hall, 2008), p. 290.

9. Ibid., p. 285.

10. Bowell and Kemp, *Critical Thinking—A Concise Guide*, p. 23.

11. Baronett, *Logic*, p. 285.

12. http://skepdic.com/refuge/ctlessons/lesson5.html, accessed on 6 April 2009.

13. http://www.daltonator.net/durandal/creationism/fallacies.shtml, accessed on 6 April 2009.

14. http://home.att.net/~tangents/issue/think/fallacy.htm#unwarranted, accessed on 6 April 2009.

15. Ibid.

16. Baronett's *Logic*, p. 295.

17. http://www.nizkor.org/features/fallacies/slippery-slope.html, accessed on 6 April 2009.

18. http://home.att.net/~tangents/issue/think/fallacy.htm#unwarranted, accessed on 6 April 2009.

19. http://www.nizkor.org/features/fallacies/gamblers-fallacy.html, accessed on 6 April 2009.

20. http://en.wikipedia.org/wiki/Non_sequitur_(logic), accessed on 6 April 2009.

21. http://home.att.net/~tangents/issue/think/fallacy.htm#unwarranted, accessed on 6 April 2009.

22. Trudy Govier, *A Practical Study of Argument* (Belmont, California: Wadsworth Publishing Company, 1992), p. 147.

4

INFORMATION AND ITS EVALUATION

But if thought is to become the possession of many, not the privilege of the few, we must have done with fear. It is fear that holds men back—fear lest their cherished beliefs should prove delusions, fear lest the institutions by which they live should prove harmful, fear lest they themselves should prove less worthy of respect than they have supposed themselves to be.

***—Bertrand Russell*[1]**

During times of universal deceit, telling the truth becomes a revolutionary act.

***—George Orwell*[2]**

4.1 Introduction

When constructing and reconstructing persuasive arguments to support a claim, we must gather the right kind of information. This is not an easy process and we can face problems both in gathering and effectively using this information—problems that emanate from psychological or social contexts. We are all social individuals who grow up in certain social and cultural settings. Our beliefs as well as our intellects develop within this socio-cultural context. We each have a unique perspective that is also a result of our socio-cultural evolution, due to which we may see or fail to see certain things.

For instance, take the case of the following symbol:

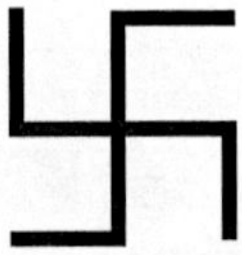

Figure 4.1 The swastika

In Hinduism, this is the swastika symbol, an auspicious symbol of well being. Therefore, to most Indian students, this symbol will hold a special meaning as there are certain positive socio-cultural emotions they associate with it. However, for European students in particular and Western students in general, this symbol has a totally different meaning. The reverse swastika as we all know is the stigmatised Nazi icon, which for most people symbolises the awful atrocities associated with Nazism. Thus, what an Indian would see when she looks at this symbol is vastly different from what a Western student would. This example shows how what we understand and what we see are largely influenced by our socio-cultural backgrounds.

Here is another example: At one time, Indians living under British rule would look upon the Union Jack as a symbol of oppression, but today it is simply the British flag for them. This shows that even though we might be exposed to the same data, we may not always draw the same information or inference from it.

What are the factors that determine our extraction of information from mere data? Is there any such thing as mere data or has everything we are exposed to already been conceptualised by us in and through our individual conceptual schemes? All these questions are discussed in mainstream philosophy.

Here, we will not consider all the details of these philosophical issues. We will however study the sources and evaluation of information.

4.2 Sources of Information

We are continuously bombarded with information. We see things, hear things, touch things, feel things, and with each observation we make, we gather data and sift out information. On a minute-by-minute basis, we receive the largest amount of information through *perception from our senses*. However, we also gather information in other ways. For instance, we may learn new things by analysing and forging connections between what we already know. In other words, we infer new information from information gathered in the past. So *inference* is one way of gathering information. Lastly, we also gather information from others who we consider as experts on subjects we do not know about. In other words, we gather information from *testimony*.

We shall consider all these sources of information and also discuss the possible hindrances to achieving information through these sources. Of course, of these three sources, we have already discussed the second one—inferences—in our discussion on arguments in the third chapter. In this chapter, therefore, we concentrate on perception and testimony as sources of information.

4.2.1 Perception as a Source of Information

People often say, "seeing is believing". But, can we always believe what we see? Consider this well-known fact from a science textbook:

Figure 4.2 The bent stick illusion

Each time we see a straight stick half immersed in water, it appears to be bent, but do we believe what we see? It is interesting that no matter how well we know that the stick is not bent and simply appears to be so when immersed in water, we continue to see it as bent. These two phenomena together force philosophers to make a distinction between *appearance* and *reality*.[3] It is commonly believed that in perception we get to know the world immediately. It is thought as though the world presents itself in its true guise in perception. If this is true, then how is it that we have illusory or hallucinatory perceptual experiences? Is perception truly a *window to the world* or can it be deceptive? This is the problem of perception.

Consider another illusion, known as the Muller Lyer Illusion:

Figure 4.3 Muller Lyer illusion

Though the sticks are equal in length, the one below appears longer than the other. However, we do not believe the trick our eyes play on us. Therefore, in this case too, we do not believe what we see and we do not see what we believe.

Here is a famous drawing:

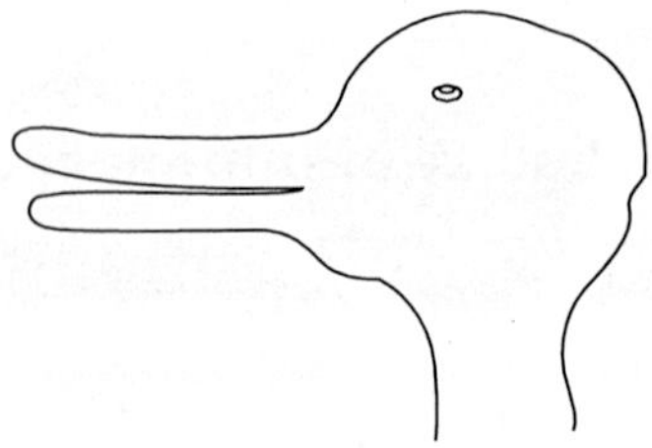

Figure 4.4 The duck-rabbit

Is this a drawing of a duck or a rabbit? That depends entirely on your perspective.

Often we see the same thing differently in different *contexts*. The example of the swastika, which we mentioned earlier, demonstrates this.

Sometimes, *expectation* directs us to see or hear certain things.

What we hear is also often not what in fact was said but what we expected to hear. An example of this can be seen in Chris Swoyer's *Critical Reasoning* where a sentence with a missing phoneme is provided: " … eel was on the _____." It was seen that when the gap is replaced with the word "axle", we assume the word with the missing phoneme was "wheel"; when the gap is replaced with "shoe" then we hear "heel"; when the gap is replaced with "orange" then we hear "peel".

Emotions also often play tricks on us and we end up seeing what we feel like seeing and omitting what we do not. I take two classic examples. The first one is again taken from Chris Swoyer's *Critical Reasoning*:

> In a classic study from the 1950s Albert Hastorf and Hadley Cantril examined biases and their effect on perception. In 1951 Dartmouth and Princeton met on the football field. The game was unusually rough, and there were several injuries and many penalties on both sides. After the game, partisans of both teams were upset. When Hastorf and Cantril asked two groups of students, one from each university, which team started the dirty play, the groups from the two universities gave quite different answers. Of course they may have heard about the game from someone else, so to study the effects of actually watching the game, Hastorf and Cantril asked a group of boosters of each school to watch a film of the game and record each penalty they noticed. Princeton boosters saw many more Dartmouth penalties than Dartmouth boosters did. Here again expectations influenced perception. But in this case peoples' expectations were influenced by which school they identified with.[4]

The second example is the story narrated in Akira Kurosawa's famous film *Rashomon*. In the film, the story of a woman's rape and the apparent murder of her husband is narrated by four different witnesses. The stories the witnesses tell vary from each other, and it is difficult for the viewer to determine which one is telling the truth. What the director shows is that because each of the witnesses had his or her own unique emotions attached to the event, none of them were lying but each one in fact perceived the same situation differently.

Perception often involves *inferences* of the kind involved in induction, wherein we leap from what is given to something new or not given. The Necker Cube shown below demonstrates this best:

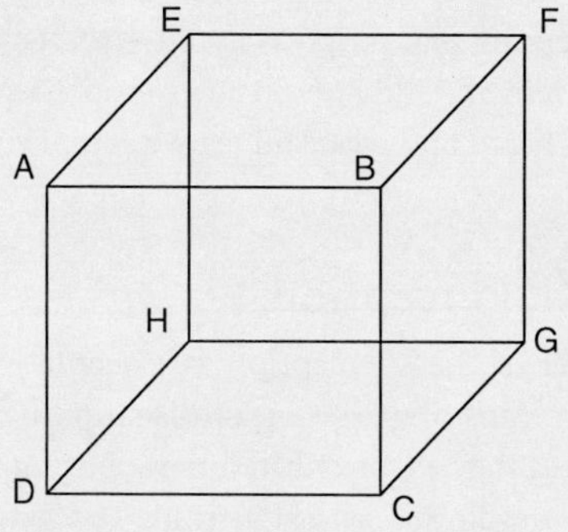

Figure 4.5 The Necker cube

This figure is in fact two-dimensional, but it looks like a three-dimensional cube. This is because we infer the presence of the third dimension from the visual data that is provided by the figure. However, in doing so, we may either feel the front face of the cube is the square ABCD or the square EFGH.

We often *read* things in a meaningful way even though what we read may make little sense. For instance, this can occur while reading what we think are intelligible words, when what we are looking at are in fact only similar in shape and form to words. A popular example of this is a paragraph that consists of gibberish words, and yet we are able to read it and make sense of what is written:

> I cdnuolt blveiee taht I cluod aulaclty uesdnatnrd waht I was rdanieg.
>
> The phaonmneal pweor of the hmuan mnid! Aoccdrnig to a rscheearch at Cmabrigde Uinervtisy, it deosn't mttaer in waht oredr the ltteers in a wrod are, the olny iprmoatnt tihng is taht the frist and lsat ltteer be in the rghit pclae. The rset can be a taotl mses and you can sitll raed it wouthit a porbelm. Tihs is bcuseae the huamn mnid deos not raed ervey lteter by istlef, but the wrod as a wlohe. Amzanig huh? Yaeh, and I awlyas thought slpeling was ipmorantt.

The problems with perception that all these cases demonstrate can be summarised in the following way:

- Everything is not as it appears to be.
- Things look different if we look at them from a different perspective.

- ❑ Sometimes we may fail to see something that another person can see.
- ❑ What we see is dependent on the context in which we see it.
- ❑ What we see is also dependent upon what we expect to see.
- ❑ What we see is also dependent upon what we desire to see.
- ❑ What we see is also dependent upon what we infer while seeing it.
- ❑ We often read gibberish or characters similar to words as meaningful words.

Every time we read something that purports itself to be the hard truth, like a newspaper report for instance, we must remember that even a newspaper report is just a record of what one reporter thought he saw, heard and felt. And yet we accept such accounts as an accurate depiction of events.

4.2.2 Problems with Perception

Another point to remember is that perception is extremely important in science, as observation is the accepted means of gathering information in a scientific enterprise. Yet the problems with perception that we have listed before bring into question the veracity of observation. We need to develop a critical attitude towards perception. In doing so, we should keep in mind the following points:

Intellectual responsibility: We do not merely perceive, we draw information from perception. Perception is an intellectual activity, and as with all intellectual activities, we should exercise intellectual responsibility while we sift out information from perceptual data. Sometimes, background knowledge helps us in doing so. For instance, our background knowledge that the stick immersed in water is in fact straight enables us to question what we see.

Rational responsibility: To infer information from what we see, we must exercise reason. But sometimes we think we have reasons for our convictions but we do not really have reasons that would justify those beliefs. So, we need to differentiate good reasons from bad ones. For example, if a friend who is six feet tall appears short to me, I should use my rational capacities and deduce that it is because he is standing at a distance from me.

Eye for relevance: We should be able to sift what is relevant from everything that we see. For example, a detective can recognise and focus on only the clues that help him solve his case when he visits the scene of a crime. We who lack the keen eye of a detective will fail to spot them among all the data presented to us.

Looking beyond the obvious: What we glean through the act of perception should in fact help us go beyond what we are merely seeing before. This was what Sherlock Holmes was good at doing. Let us have a classic example from *The Study in Scarlet.* This is what went between Holmes and Watson when they were on a camping trip.

> Holmes said, "Watson, look up. What do you see?"
> "Well, I see thousands of stars."

"And what does that mean to you?"

"Well, I suppose it means that of all the planets and suns and moons in the universe, that we are truly the one most blessed with the reason to deduce theorems to make our way in this world of criminal enterprises and blind greed. It means that we are truly small in the eyes of God but struggle each day to be worthy of the senses and spirit we have been blessed with. And, I suppose, at the very least, in the meteorological sense, it means that it is most likely that we will have another nice day tomorrow. What does it mean to you, Holmes?"

"To me, it means someone has stolen our tent." [5]

Sensitivity to context: The context in which we see something can influence the way in which we see it. For instance, the first line in the Muller Lyer Illusion appears shorter because the arrow heads point inwards, while the second line looks longer because we view it in the context of the arrow heads pointing outwards.

Recognising and checking emotional biases: We have seen how our emotional biases can distort our vision. We should be able to handle these biases well and recognise that what we see can be a consequence of these biases. We should then be able to go beyond these biases. One way to do this is to question everything that we dogmatically hold to be true.

4.3 Testimony as a Source of Information

There are many things in the world to which we do not have any access. In order to gather information about such things, we need to rely on the words of others i.e., other people's testimony. For instance, we cannot know what is happening in Antarctica but we rely on experts who tell us that the ice is gradually melting there as a result of global warming, which in turn is causing sea levels all over the world to rise. If I need to know which notes are used in the Rāga Bhairavi, I need to ask an expert in Indian classical music. When we want to know what is wrong with our body, we go to a physician. If we want to know when the monsoon will arrive, we ask a meteorologist. If we want to know what is wrong with our car, we go to a motor mechanic. Thus, we are constantly relying on other people's authority for information. However, it is important to exercise extreme caution when we take other people's words as authoritative.

Some of the problems we can encounter when deriving information from what people say have already been mentioned in the previous chapter in our discussion on fallacies. We must be especially careful when drawing inferences when others' words have lexical and syntactic ambiguity. In such cases, we must make efforts to understand exactly what they are saying. Caution must also be exercised when their words contain vague terms so that we do not commit the fallacy of Appeal to Inappropriate Authority. Let us study this in detail and try to understand when we can take someone else's words as authoritative and glean information from them.

I will start by citing an example from everyday life. In a court case, we see that witnesses provide evidence, and it is on the basis of this evidence that the lawyer deduces who was guilty. The court might either be satisfied by the lawyer's argument or not. The verdict will depend entirely upon the credibility of the evidence provided and the acceptability of the logical connections that the lawyer makes with the evidence and his proposed conclusion. So we see how *what other people say may well become the premises of the arguments we make* in order to further our knowledge.

What other people say also constitutes the background information that is necessary for us to make inferences. This background information substantiates the premises and also helps us to make the necessary logical connections in order to arrive at a conclusion. For instance, suppose you want to vote for or against a motion for setting up an automobile company on cultivable land belonging to some farmers. You will need background information about the economic losses the farmers would suffer in case of the development, information about the effect such a company would have on your state's overall development and economy, information on the number of jobs that would be generated if the company were to be set up etc. Such background information will definitely be based on the testimony of experts in this field and will be used by you to decide whether you should support the establishment of the automobile company. You will also use such testimony to evaluate arguments presented by all relevant parties for or against the setting up of the company. Thus, the "evaluation of arguments often requires background knowledge obtained from testimony".[6]

The most important task when evaluating information given by others is to first evaluate their expertise. In doing so, to begin with, we have to be able to distinguish an expert from a quack or charlatan. Next, we should be able to decide what to do when people whom we have identified as experts differ in their opinion on the same issue. This problem is more difficult to tackle. We call someone or something (objects like encyclopaedias and online resources) an expert or authority when they possess a large amount of knowledge or information on a particular issue or when they have had a lot of experience in something. For instance, a seismologist is an expert on earthquakes because she has read about and studied earthquakes, but an illiterate farmer who has lived through many earthquakes throughout his life might well be an expert as well. If I want to know something about a philosophical concept, I would log onto the Stanford Encyclopaedia of Philosophy, which is on the Internet. Thus, experts may be people with special knowledge or people with special experience. This is why mothers more often consult their own mothers instead of paediatricians when bringing up their children.

There are a few things that we have to remember about experts, especially in today's day when we derive a lot of information from the Internet. First, *experts are not immune to error*; they can make mistakes, but that does not mean they have lost their expertise in the matter. Another thing to remember is that there are degrees of expertise. We may have five expert eye surgeons in a hospital but not all of their expertise would be to the same degree—one of them might be more of an expert than the others, having knowledge on some novel techniques and more experience. Another point to remember is that a person may be an expert in one field and not in another related field. For example, not all eye surgeons may be experts in performing cataract surgeries. Below are the points we should keep in mind when evaluating the information provided to us by experts:[7]

i. Authority
ii. Objectivity
iii. Accuracy
iv. Coverage
v. Relevance
vi. Time Aspects
vii. Usability
viii. Sources

According to this list, we first judge whether the person in question is an expert on the issue at hand. Second, we must try to judge whether the expert's claims are objective. One of the ways in which we can judge this is by analysing the language the person uses. We must not consider the person's claims objective if the language she uses is too emotional, persuasive and filled with rhetoric ploys. We must also try to find out if the person has any vested interests. For example, suppose we read a report written by a physician in which he recommends a particular vitamin tablet. Before taking his advice and purchasing the tablet, we should see if the physician is perhaps receiving a payment from the drug company manufacturing it. Whenever we encounter any information in the newspaper, on the Internet or on television, we must see who is providing the information. Is it the state? Is it a media group with some political allegiance? These are the things we must be careful about.

While judging the accuracy of information, we must ensure we see the following:[8]

- ❑ Explanation of the methods used to obtain the information
- ❑ Listing of reference sources used
- ❑ Evidence that the content was reviewed by other authorities for accuracy
- ❑ Information on how studies were conducted and analysed
- ❑ A lack of obvious errors or omissions
- ❑ A lack of spelling, grammatical and typographical errors
- ❑ Visible care taken to detect all of these problems and avoid content errors

We must also keep an eye on the coverage of the information. That is, we have to see if all the things that are in question have been addressed by the information provided.

We need to see if the information provided is relevant for the issue at hand. In other words, we should see if we need the information at all. We must also see if it is practically applicable, useful and whether we can use the information for our purpose. In short, we must see if the information has utility for us.

The time aspect of the information provided by a person, a book, newspaper, report or web page is also extremely important. There are new developments in every field almost on a daily basis and so it is important to know when some information was provided in order to check if it is up to date.

When gathering written information, we must see if all the source material has been indicated and if they are all credible sources. All of this is not only relevant when considering information we get from others but all kinds of information, especially information we read. This will be discussed in detail in the next chapter.

Chris Swoyer mentions seven questions that we need to ask when we are evaluating another's testimony or some source of information:

1. Do we care enough about this issue to try to evaluate the likelihood that a given source about it is accurate? The general point here is the same whether the potential source is a world-class expert or just someone we meet on the street. But the costs of getting information from someone you know or encounter may be lower than the costs of getting information from an expert, so it may be reasonable to collect more information from those around you.
2. Is the issue one in which anyone can really be relied on to know the facts? The point here is the same regardless of the source. If there are no experts in the field, then there is little likelihood that your friends and acquaintances will be particularly good sources of information about it.
3. Is the source generally right about this sort of issue? Perhaps Anne has always given good advice on fixing computers, while Sam has often been wrong. Sally has always provided good advice about who to go out with, while Wilbur's advice is hopeless.
4. Is the issue one where people would mostly agree? If there is little agreement among others about something, you are on your own.
5. Is the source's claim very unusual or surprising? The point here is the same regardless of the source. If a claim is sufficiently unlikely it is more probable that the source is wrong than that the claim is true.
6. Is there any reason to think that the source might be biased or mistaken in this particular case? Sally is a good judge of people and full of insights about their personalities, but she has a blind spot about Burt. Bill usually gives good advice, but he's really been stressed out lately. John saw the car I asked about, but it was dark and he could have made a mistake about its license number. Indeed, as we will see later in this module, even honest eyewitnesses are much less reliable than people commonly suppose.
7. Has the source been quoted accurately? Hank tells us that Sally said that Cindy and Paul are back together again. Is there any reason to think Hank might be getting it wrong?

We shall now specify some safeguards we need to follow in order to not get misled by other people's words. After identifying what is relevant for us, we must assess the arguments that are presented. We must check the reliability of the source. We must gather information on the issue at hand from more than one independent source. We must also be cautious about the intentions of the source, see if he or she has any vested interest in the matter or if he or she is likely to mislead us for some reason. We must also see if there could be any reason for or possibility of the expert making a mistake in the matter. To evaluate the information better, we may also start reading up on the issue ourselves, learning about it and trying to develop a certain amount of expertise in it. We must see the issue at hand from as many perspectives as possible.

KEY POINTS

Sources of information

- **Perception:**
- Though perception is the most common source of information and the one that is regarded as most reliable, there are certain precautions that should be taken while drawing information from perception:

    i. Everything is not as it appears to be
    ii. Things appear different if we look at them from a different perspective
    iii. Sometimes, we may fail to see something that another person can see
    iv. What we see is dependent on the context in which we see it
    v. What we see is also dependent upon what we expect to see
    vi. What we see is also dependent upon what we desire to see
    vii. What we see is also dependent upon what we infer while seeing it
    viii. We often read gibberish thinking it consists of meaningful words although it may only appear similar to actual words

- **Testimony:**

There are a great many things that we learn from others, especially from what others say or write. We need to keep in mind that we can accept information transmitted from others only when we are sure that the person is an expert and is honestly trying to give us genuine information. We must also remember that in spite of being an expert, he or she may go wrong. We must therefore cautiously evaluate the information given by keeping an eye on:

i. Authority
ii. Objectivity
iii. Accuracy
iv. Coverage
v. Relevance
vi. Time Aspects
vii. Usability
viii. Sources

THINKING THROUGH EXERCISE 1

i. What are the different sources of information?
ii. Is seeing believing? If not, why not?
iii. What are the things we have to keep in mind when we receive perceptual information?
iv. What do perceptual illusions teach us?
v. What are the problems of receiving knowledge by testimony?
vi. Who is an expert? How do we evaluate information gathered from an expert's testimony?

4.4 Reason and Basic Human Limitations

We have seen by now that in evaluating information as well as in taking a decision or forming an opinion on any issue, we need to carefully exercise reason. There may be many different kinds of hindrances to evaluating information in particular and critical thinking in general. Some of these hindrances have their roots in some basic human limitations while others have their roots in our social condition. First, we will consider the hindrances resulting from basic human limitations. These are as follows:[9]

i. Confirmation bias and selective thinking

Human beings have a tendency to notice only those things that confirm their beliefs and to overlook or give less importance to things that contradict their beliefs. As an illustration of this point, we may quote Tolstoy on the subject of confirmation bias from his 1897 article, "What is Art?": "I know that most men, including those at ease with problems of the greatest complexity, can seldom accept the simplest and most obvious truth if it be such as would oblige them to admit the falsity of conclusions which they have proudly taught to others, and which they have woven, thread by thread, into the fabrics of their life." It is due to this essay that confirmation bias is often called the Tolstoy Syndrome.

Let us consider an example. Suppose Ranjana believes that if a cat crosses your path, you meet with an accident. To confirm this belief, she will find out about all such instances when someone has met with an accident after a cat has crossed his or her path. The safeguard we can exercise is with regard to the information we get. What we must do is objectively analyse and evaluate *all* the relevant information and view it from *all* possible perspectives.

ii. False memories and confabulation

We often face a problem when we need to remember past events. There are usually bits and pieces that we cannot remember. What we usually do in such cases is confabulate, that is, we unconsciously fill in the gaps by fabricating fantasies. Let us consider an example from a practice in criminal investigation. When a witness is asked to recognise the perpetrator of a crime from a line-up, the policemen never give the witness a picture of the accused because this might cloud the witness' memory. The greatest caution one can exercise here is being sceptical about one's own memory.

iii. Ignorance

We as human beings have only a limited repertoire and we are often ignorant of many important facts. Due to our lack of background knowledge on certain subjects, we might end up making incorrect judgements. For instance, people thought small pox was caused by a curse until a scientist provided them with the facts. One should develop an enquiring attitude and study the issue at hand before making a judgement. In cases where one lacks the relevant knowledge, one should simply refrain from making a judgement at all.

iv. Limitations of perception

We have previously discussed this topic during our discussion on perception as a source of information. It is important to be aware of one's perceptual limitations. We must not believe in our senses dogmatically. Although this is not something we do often, we sometimes fall into the trap of accepting whatever we see. Should we believe that the sun is the same size as the moon because one's shadow perfectly covers the other? Astronomy has taught us that the sizes of moon and sun are not the same but a solar eclipse occurs when the moon goes in front of the sun and blocks most of the sun's light from the earth.

v. Personal biases and prejudices

We all have personal biases and prejudices that significantly overshadow our reason, hampering us from thinking objectively and critically. For instance, some religious people refuse to see the truth of scientific research. On the other hand, some people consumed by science fail to see the emotional side of certain issues. We must develop the ability to view things from different sides and perspectives in order to overcome our biases and prejudices.

vi. Physical and emotional hindrances

Often, when someone is under extreme physical duress, like suffering from a disease, stress, fatigue or is under the influence of some drug, they might fail to see things properly, think properly or understand properly. A rational person ought to exercise extreme restraint in making any judgements when under such physical duress.

vii. Testimonial evidence

We have already discussed how we often take other people's words as true without reasoning through what they say. Sometimes we do this because we might just be impressed by the person's charismatic personality or by his title or his authoritative manner. We must avoid being led astray by such confidence tricksters.

KEY POINTS

Reason and basic human limitations

Human beings are subject to certain basic human limitations that stand in their way of becoming good critical thinkers. These limitations are as follows:

i. Confirmation Bias and Selective Thinking
ii. False Memories and Confabulation
iii. Ignorance
iv. Perception Limitations
v. Personal Biases and Prejudices
vi. Physical and Emotional Hindrances
vii. Testimonial Evidence

THINKING THROUGH EXERCISE 2

i. What do we mean by basic human limitations?
ii. What are the basic human limitations?

4.5 Reason and Social Influences

Human beings have evolved and survived as a species because as a group humans have depended extensively on social mechanisms that have helped them flourish and live. One of the reasons for human evolution is the hierarchical nature of the social structure with which they have grown and lived. This is why we have almost a natural tendency to conform to our peers, follow our leaders and obey and live within societal norms. These are matters of socio-biological inheritance. We are deeply influenced by society but are almost completely unaware of these influences. Some of the power groups of our society have taken advantage of this and have exercised great control over our thought patterns. These social influences have nourished us in many ways but have also impeded our healthy critical thinking.

Let us now discuss the impact of social influences on our rational activities. We often find that even people who are otherwise extremely able critical thinkers are sometimes unable to detect or resist such impeding social influences. Often, we find that a charismatic leader is able to manipulate the thoughts of an intelligent social group, which in turn causes serious problems not only for individuals but also for families, communities, religious organisations, business houses and even political systems. One clear example of this is the social influence of the Nazi ideology over a large section of German people during the World War II. Even aside from such extreme examples, there are social forces that deeply influence our thoughts regarding gender, religion, culture, ethnicity, race, economic status, education etc. In spite of all our efforts to think for ourselves, we are almost powerless before the coercion of social forces. One of the reasons why we are so helplessly swayed by these forces is that

> Most of the knowledge we have was acquired from others. Most of the goods we own were made by others. In a diverse, highly technological society like ours, we continually have to rely on the expert opinions of others. And the most important things in life for most of us are our relationships with other people.[10]

We know that in critical thinking, we are concerned with methods of persuasion. Of course, not all persuasions are rational persuasions. We often find the need to persuade people to do something that we ourselves have almost no rational way of doing. In such situations, we use other means of persuasion. In our society, there are even people who persuade others for a living. In fact, the whole business of advertising is about persuading people to buy things.

As is obvious from the example of advertising, there are some very effective and subtle techniques of convincing people through means that are not purely rational. We must remember that such techniques often involve manipulation, which consists of irrational methods of persuasion. For instance, we may get someone to accept something by first pleasing the person with undue praise. Perhaps a little child first kisses and hugs his mother, tells her how much he loves her and when his mother is completely overcome with emotion, he says he doesn't feel like doing his homework. Parents on the other hand sometimes use what is known as paternalistic persuasion by saying things like, "My son should not go abroad to study because he is still a child and I know what is best for him."

Whenever we manipulate a person to think in a certain way or decide what we want them to, we prevent them from thinking for themselves. What we are doing is taking the right to decide and think things for themselves away from people. This is not only unfair but also dangerous. If we do not give people this right, we do them two injustices—we deny them of their right and we also stop them from taking the responsibility of taking independent decisions. This is a problem that many parents bring upon themselves by being overprotective of their children and excessively controlling them. This either ends up in a breakdown of the relationship between the parents and the children or sadly ends in the children never quite growing up to be responsible individuals. Parents manage to do all this because they have a kind of social and psychological control over their children.

Of course, this is not only true of parents. Our social and political leaders who hold a position of authority over us, even the media that has an amazing control over us, often do quite the same thing—manipulate our thoughts. Each time a fast food company issues an advertisement of a free popular cartoon toy being offered along with their product, for instance, a tremendous desire is created in the minds of children who in turn coax and cajole their parents to buy the product. As soon as one parent does this, there is tremendous peer pressure for the other parents of the child's friends to do the same.

Advertisers or parents might use arguments that are persuasive but are often fallacious, as we have noticed in the third chapter.

4.6 Means of Social Influences

We shall now discuss the many ways in which society influences our beliefs, behaviour, decisions and attitudes. They are as follows:[11]

i. Socialisation

Children develop through socialising. Socialisation starts at a very early age within the family, then in school and then in the world at large. The picture of the world that we have is largely a machination of this socialisation process. As young children, we do not have the resources to question all the ideas and ideologies that we are fed day in and day out. The linguistic or rational repertoire necessary for one to argue and think through the ideas that are fed to us are just not available to children. Children consequently are entirely at the receiving end. They not only do what they are told but also come to believe that doing what their parents and teachers say is right and doing everything else is wrong. They venture into the world through their efforts to conform with the social norms first set by their family, then by their educators and friends, then the media, society, their ethnic group, religious group and so on. Chris Swoyer says,

> Think of the beliefs that are most important to you. They are likely to include beliefs about things like religion, morality, patriotism, and love. Can you recall a time when someone reasoned with you and got you to change your mind about these matters? Did you ever seriously entertain the thought that some religious or moral views quite different from your own might be true and that yours might be false?[12]

We are in many ways what the society that has nurtured us has made us. What are the safeguards that a critical thinker has to exercise to prevent these social influences from overshadowing her ability to think critically? The answer is, we must develop the ability to see things from different perspectives. For instance, we could imagine what it would be like if we had been born into an altogether different society and what our views would then be.

ii. Experts

As we have already discussed, we often rely on experts in order to gather information on issues that fall outside our scope of knowledge. Sometimes, we even accept the words of experts blindly. However, we must remember that experts too can make mistakes. We should, as we have already discussed, be able to judge who is and who is not an expert.

iii. The mere presence of others

Often, our behaviour is affected either positively or negatively by the presence of other people. For instance, we sometimes sing better, play better, work better, make better presentations and perform better when we have an audience. It might also happen that in the presence of certain people, our performance is hampered. In the presence of a teacher who seems scary to a child, for instance, the child might fail to perform in the way that he would if a different teacher were present. A cricket team often performs better in front of its home crowd than on foreign soil.

iv. Persuasion

We shall now discuss how in society there are many professional persuaders whose sole purpose is to persuade us to act according to their wishes. We must remember that the most effective and successful ways of persuasion are those in which the person at the receiving end does not even notice that she is being persuaded. A person who is trying to convince an expert in a selection committee to choose candidate X, for instance, might overtly try to convince the experts about a less impressive and less qualified candidate. And when candidate X comes for the interview, the expert automatically becomes positively disposed to her without knowing that it is in fact the persuader's surreptitious persuasion skills at work. There are many techniques of persuasion. Chris Swoyer discusses some of these techniques in detail in his book:

- The Foot-in-the-Door Technique, in which the persuader asks someone to first agree to something small and then later makes a bigger request.
- The Low-balling Technique, in which the persuader gets a person to buy or invest in something by providing inaccurate information about its price. For example, a real estate agent often compels you to book a flat quoting a low price and later asks for more, knowing you can do nothing at that stage as you have already committed.
- The Door-in-the-Face Technique, which is the opposite of the Foot-in-the-Door Technique. In this technique, the persuader first tries to convince you about something big. When you refuse, the persuader gets you to agree to something small, which in fact was his intention all along.

v. Prejudices and stereotypes

The dictionary meaning of the word "stereotype" is "a conventional, formulaic, and over-simplified conception, opinion, or image".[13] When we hold a somewhat oversimplified view about a group or class of people, we are turning them into stereotypes. For example, stereotypically, feminists are regarded as men haters. Stereotypes emerge within our social structure, and if we look into the history of human civilisation, we will see how stereotypes have done great harm. A stereotypical attitude always involves a hateful "Us vs. Them" mentality. We can take again the example of the Holocaust in which there was an attempted and partially successful annihilation of European Jews by the Nazis who had stereotyped Jews in a way that was officially sanctioned by the governmental machinery.

We must realise that stereotypes are dangerous in too many ways. First of all, stereotypes result from prejudices of a certain section of people against another section. It is a result of extreme intolerance. Secondly, if we do not check our prejudices then we will become discriminating, intolerant and may even become violent. This in the Nazi case led to genocide. We also notice that in the Nazi case, the prejudice was spread among the common people by use of propaganda by demagogues. This sort of propaganda totally dehumanises the victim group.

A critical thinker should avoid all kinds of stereotypes. Here, we should mention a beautiful example of social stereotypes being ignored by a spiritual leader. Jesus broke all stereotypical prejudices when he associated with prostitutes and lepers. Mahatma Gandhi and B. R. Ambedkar too dispelled social prejudices and brought *dalits* into the fold of civil society, a position they were traditionally denied due to the stereotype associated with them.

vi. Conformity

As we have said before, as children we learn to conform by the social and ethical norms we are taught by our parents, teachers, peers and even the media. Each one of us has the desire to be socially accepted and to be socially praised. This itself acts as a pressure. Chris Swoyer calls this "informational influence" and "normative influence". We begin to think like others think. We regard as right that which others think is right. Swoyer writes, "Normative influences can lead people to conform publicly, but they may not privately accept the views."

vii. Obedience

This is possibly one of the most interesting aspects of social influences on critical thinking. Within a social framework, we curiously obey diktats that we do not at heart agree with. A path-breaking study on this was conducted by Stanley Milgram. The famous Milgram Experiment was a set of social psychology experiments that were conducted in order to measure the willingness of people to obey an authoritative figure who ordered them to do things that they did not approve of themselves.

The experiment involved three people. The first is E or the experimenter who holds some amount of authority over the second group, which is T, or the teacher, and L, the learner. The E orders T to ask L some questions and give him or her electric shocks whenever L makes a mistake. In order to convince T the shocks are real and painful, he or she is given a sample electric shock from the shock generator he is about to use on his student. In actuality, T's action produces no electric shock; the shock generator is however connected to an audio tape on which L is previously recorded expressing sounds of pain to lead T to believe that the shocks are real. At the onset of the experiment, T is instructed to increase the shock level if L makes more mistakes. As the mistakes become more in number and the shock level rises, T shows signs of extreme stress—first T becomes nervous, then wants to stop the experiment, then wants to know the purpose of the experiment. When T really wants to stop the experiment, E gives him the following orders in this sequence:

i. Please continue.
ii. The experiment requires that you continue.

iii. It is absolutely essential that you continue.
iv. You have no other choice, you *must* go on.
v. Go on or else.

If T wanted to stop even after the fifth order, the experiment would be stopped. But if any T continued then the fake shock meter would depict its voltage as being to the maximum.

What is remarkable is that contrary to anybody's expectation, 65 per cent of people on whom this experiment was conducted actually went on to give their Ls what they believed were the maximum shock levels. This finding has far-reaching social, psychological and ethical relevance.

After conducting the experiment, Milgram came up with two theories that could explain the results of his experiment and also could say something significant about the nature of obedience within the social context. Let us briefly state the two theories Milgram proposed:[14]

- Theory of Conformism:
  "A subject who has neither ability nor expertise to make decisions, especially in a crisis, will leave decision making to the group and its hierarchy. The group is the person's behavioral model."
- Agentic State Theory:
  The "essence of obedience consists in the fact that a person comes to view himself as the instrument for carrying out another person's wishes, and he therefore no longer sees himself as responsible for his actions. Once this critical shift of viewpoint has occurred in the person, all of the essential features of obedience follow."

KEY POINTS

Reason and social influences

Human beings are social animals. They are born and raised within a social milieu whose influences both nourish and cripple them. Certain social influences are beneficial while others are often detrimental to the development of critical thinkers. These are:

i. Socialisation
ii. Experts
iii. The Mere Presence of Others
iv. Persuasion
v. Prejudice and Stereotypes
vi. Conformity
vii. Obedience

THINKING THROUGH EXERCISE 3

i. Why is human thought influenced by society?
ii. What are the means of social influence?

4.7 Concluding Remarks

We have discussed in this chapter the different sources of information and unique hindrances that people face in gathering, understanding and evaluating information. By way of a conclusion, we may present a few words on the general attitude that a critical thinker needs to develop in order to circumvent these hindrances and take control of his or her own mind.

First of all, whenever we address an issue, we must be clear on what we want to achieve by addressing it. We then have to take an active interest in gathering all the relevant information about that issue. While doing so, we need to look for reliable resources and evaluate and re-evaluate them. Once we have gathered the information, we must avoid making hasty generalisations that are inaccurate and biased. We should not complicate simple things and must not simplify complicated things. We should be open to different opinions and perspectives and consider each opinion with the same degree of seriousness and academic honesty. We should always be open to change and new ideas. We should withhold our judgements when we are not sufficiently informed or not sure. We should not accept an opinion simply because it comes from an authority—we should always critically assess opinions and orders even when they come from our experts or seniors. We should have an equally critical attitude towards our own ideas and should test them from time to time. We must also avoid any kind of stereotypical thinking. When we arrive at some other point of view by our own analysis, we should accept it with an open mind. In other words, we must always keep in mind that we too can make mistakes.

4.8 More Exercises

1. How does the bent stick illusion prove that seeing is not believing? What do we learn about perceptual knowledge from this example?
2. How does the Muller Lyer Illusion demonstrate a distinction between how things appear to us and how they really are?
3. Explain how perception is perspectival with the help of the duck-rabbit illusion.
4. How does the Necker Cube illusion demonstrate that there are inferences involved in certain perceptual processes?

5. Why do we need to rely on experts to gain information?
6. How do we decide who is an expert in a field?
7. What are the eight things we need to check when we evaluate information gathered from the words of others?
8. What are the basic human limitations?
9. What do we mean by "conformation bias and selective thinking"?
10. What do we mean by "false memories and confabulation"?
11. What do we mean by "ignorance"?
12. What are the Perception Limitations?
13. What do we mean by "personal biases and prejudices"?
14. What are the physical and emotional hindrances to critical thinking?
15. What are the social influences on reason?
16. What is the role of socialisation in thinking?
17. What is the role of experts in thinking?
18. How does the mere presence of others influence our thoughts and actions?
19. What is the role of persuasion in thinking?
20. How do prejudices and stereotypes act as hindrances to thinking for ourselves?
21. What is the role of conformity in thinking?
22. What is Milgram's Experiment? What does this experiment prove?
23. How can we as critical thinkers overcome the problems of gathering information?
24. How can we as critical thinkers overcome the problems of human limitations?
25. How can we as critical thinkers overcome the problems of social influence on thought?

NOTES AND REFERENCES

1. *The Basic Writings of Bertrand Russell* (New York, NY: Routledge, 2009).

2. George Orwell, *Nineteen Eighty-Four* (London: Secker and Warburg, 1949).

3. Recall Russell's famous chapter on "Appearance and Reality" in his *The Problem of Philosophy*. Oxford University Press paperback, Oxford, 1959.

4. Chris Swoyer, *Critical Reasoning: A User's Manual,* www.ou.edu/ouph l/faculty/chr s/ crmscreen. pdf, p. 79.

5. Arthur Conan Doyle, *The Study in Scarlet*, Penguin Classics (London: Penguin Books, 2001).

6. Chris Swoyer, *Critical Reasoning: A User's Manual* www.ou.edu/ouph l/faculty/chr s/ crmscreen. pdf, p. 87, accessed on 21 April 2009.

7. Gayle L. Wolf, https://www.msu.edu/~wolfegay/how%20to%20evaluate.htm, accessed on 21 April 2009

8. Ibid.

9. Greg R. Haskins, http://www.skepdic.com/essays/Haskins.html, accessed on 19 April 2009.

10. Chris Swoyer, *Critical Reasoning*, p. 450.

11. Ibid., p. 452.

12. Ibid., p. 454.

13. http://www.answers.com/topic/stereotype.

14. http://en.wikipedia.org/wiki/Milgram_experiment, accessed on 23 April 2003.

5

THINKING, READING, AND WRITING CRITICALLY

When you wish to instruct, be brief; that men's minds take in quickly what you say, learn its lesson, and retain it faithfully. Every word that is unnecessary only pours over the side of a brimming mind.

—*Cicero*[1]

5.1 Introduction

Now that we have had an introduction to critical thinking, we shall see how by being a critical thinker one also becomes a critical reader or learner as well as a critical writer. Before we go into this discussion, however, let us recapitulate what constitutes critical thinking:

A critical thinker is …

i. an open-minded person who is willing to address a question with an open mind. Recall the features of a critical thinker that we mentioned in the first chapter:
   - ❑ a person guided by reason
   - ❑ a person not guided just by emotion
   - ❑ a person who considers all the evidence at hand and follows the route that it points towards

- ❑ a person who is in search of the best possible explanation
- ❑ a person who is free from motives and biases
- ❑ a person who is aware of her own prejudices and is not usually influenced by them
- ❑ a person who does not think in terms of stereotypes
- ❑ a person who has a free and open mind

ii. someone who does not accept anything without asking questions about the issue and without giving the issue a serious thought

iii. someone who tries to define concepts with precision, avoiding vagueness and ambiguity

iv. a person who meets the standards of critical thinking, which pertain to:
- ❑ clarity
- ❑ accuracy
- ❑ precision
- ❑ relevance
- ❑ depth
- ❑ breadth

v. someone who rationally evaluates all evidence

vi. someone who also rationally evaluates all information

vii. a person who examines and analyses all possible assumptions and biases

viii. is someone who is able to look beyond the obvious

ix. is someone who is able to look at things from different perspectives and can present different interpretations of the same thing

x. someone who accepts that she is fallible

Having recapitulated what makes a thinker a critical thinker, we may now go on to ask how we can become critical in reading, learning and writing.

5.2 Critical Thinking, and Critical Reading and Learning

Students, teachers and other people dealing with information or knowledge on a regular basis are always gathering information from written texts and therefore need to be skilled at such work. Critical reading is a technique of doing this in the best possible way. We must of course remember that critical reading is not the same as critical thinking. Below is the difference between the two, beautifully summed up by Dan Kurland:

> Critical *reading* is a technique for *discovering* information and ideas within a text.
> Critical *thinking* is a technique for *evaluating* information and ideas, for deciding what to accept and believe.[2]

When a critical reader approaches any text, she adopts a rational attitude towards it. In this way, she approaches it with the mind of a critical thinker. She reads with great care and active interest and analyses the facts she gathers from the text. She then reflects on what she has read. A critical thinker is concerned with evidence. So her attitude towards a subject is what facilitates the work of a critical reader.

Let us consider an example of a sentence one might come across in a newspaper and see how a critical reader should approach it. We take this example from the third chapter of this book:

The government will announce that the electricity supply is to be cut off tomorrow.

We already know that this is a syntactically ambiguous sentence. A critical thinker would try to disambiguate this sentence by deciding whether this means:

Tomorrow, the government will announce that the electricity supply is to be cut off.

Or,

The government will announce that tomorrow the electricity supply is to be cut off.

The critical reader who is not so concerned with the syntactic structure as such will be concerned with what this sentence means in the context of its occurrence.

It is not very clear what comes first—critical reading or critical thinking. It is, however, quite clear that a critical thinker is most fitted to be a critical reader and a critical reader definitely demonstrates critical thinking skills. According to Dan Kurland, critical thinking and critical reading work together in harmony:

> Critical thinking allows us to monitor our understanding as we read. If we sense that assertions are ridiculous or irresponsible (critical thinking), we examine the text more closely to test our understanding (critical reading). Conversely, critical thinking depends on critical reading. You can think critically about a text (critical thinking), after all, only if you have understood it (critical reading). We may choose to accept or reject a presentation, but we must know why. We have a responsibility to ourselves, as well as to others, to isolate the real issues of agreement or disagreement. Only then can we understand and respect other people's views. To recognize and understand those views, we must read critically.

However, we must realise that critical reading has a specific aim. When we read, we evaluate what we read. For instance, when reading a book, we try to see how well it addresses the issue at hand. Of course here we are speaking about academic books and not literary works of fiction. For the evaluation of literary work, we need neither critical thinking nor critical reading. But when we are evaluating an academic work or a text from a newspaper, we look out for the following things:

- ❑ Whether the subject matter has been properly identified and discussed
- ❑ Whether all the concepts mentioned and all the terms used in the book have been well explained and clearly defined

- ❑ Whether the claims made in the book are substantiated by evidence
- ❑ Whether the causal connections claimed in the work have been proven
- ❑ Whether any exceptions to the claims made have been addressed and explained adequately
- ❑ Whether references have been made properly
- ❑ Whether the relation between the claim and our commonsensical beliefs, if any, has been addressed
- ❑ Overall, we must evaluate the information presented in the text. This includes checking ten things:
    - i. "Content
    - ii. Credibility
    - iii. Critical Thinking
    - iv. Copyright
    - v. Citation
    - vi. Continuity
    - vii. Censorship
    - viii. Connectivity
    - ix. Comparability
    - x. Context"[3]

I illustrate this point with the mention of a tradition in Indian classical philosophy. Each text on classical Indian philosophy starts with what is knows as the *Anubandha Catuṣṭaya* or the four prerequisites. *The Dictionary of Indian Philosophy* defines this as follows: "There are four preambulary factors of philosophical work: the subject matter (Viṣaya), the aim (prayojana), the relation (sambandha), and the person for whom the work is meant (adhikari)." It is customary to start every book with these four preliminaries. In order to spur the prospective reader to read through the book, the author must first state what the subject matter is. Then the author must state the aim or the goal to be achieved by the study of the subject matter at hand. Next, the aunthor must show the relation between this goal and the study of the subject matter and finally the author must mention what kind of person might be interested in reading this book or what the audience is.

I believe these points address both what is required of a critical reader as well as a *critical writer*. We shall discuss the notion of a critical writer shortly. For now, I would like to show how these four *anuvandhas* are relevant to critical reading.

When we read a book we want to know:

- i. What is the subject matter of the book?
- ii. Why is the study of this subject necessary?
- iii. What aim can be achieved by the study of this subject?
- iv. Is this an aim that I want to achieve?

Unless the author specifies these four things in clear terms, it is not worth reading the text concerned. Even if authors do not state these four preliminaries in the way classical Indian philosophical texts did, these *anuvandhas* should be clear from the text itself.

What is clear from the above discussion is that a critical reader doesn't just read. She reads in a *reflective* way. As we have already said, the critical reader does not only gather facts but also interprets. So the primary aim is not just the accumulation of information. The critical thinker has to, while reading, think about the subject for herself. This is the only way in which she can assimilate the new information she gathers within her own repertoire and internalise it. Therefore, while reading, teachers advise students to take notes, highlight key issues, list the evidence given to support the claims made in the text and examine the ways in which the claim has been argued in the text.

Below is a complete list of all the things that a critical reader must do:

i. Identify the main claim of the text in order to see how it is explained and defended
ii. Identify the purpose of the text and examine if the text serves its purpose
iii. Identify the context of the text. This involves:
   (a) Identifying the academic background of the issue being discussed
   (b) Identifying the audience for whom the text has been written
   (c) Describing the history of the subject matter
   (d) Stating the importance of all of the above points to the subject matter
iv. Identify the concepts mentioned in the text. This will involve checking whether these concepts have been properly defined in the text.
v. Identify the theories employed or assumed in the text
vi. Identify the methodology employed in the text
vii. Identify the arguments employed in the text
viii. Be sensitive to the fact that not all disciplines employ the same methodology or the same kind of argumentation
ix. Evalute how well the text does the job that it takes on

One of the main aims of reading critically is to *interpret the text* at hand. Let us try to understand what this might involve. According to Dan Kurland, when we face a text as a critical thinker, we need to concentrate on three things:

i. What a text *says: restatement*
ii. What a text *does: description*
iii. What a text *means: interpretation*[4]

The main aim of interpretation is to recognise the purpose of the author, to understand the way in which the author tries to persuade us to believe in what he or she is claiming and also to recognise the possible biases of the author. What makes reading, or to be more precise, critically reading difficult is that none of these are obvious from what is literally presented in the text (or at least not *always* obvious). This makes the job of the reader difficult as it involves *an active engagement with the subject matter*. But we may achieve this by thinking critically about the subject matter. We need to make inferences at each step. For instance, "recognizing purpose involves inferring a basis for choices of content and language".[5] In order to understand the tone of the author and to understand the modes of persuasion he or she has applied, we need to examine and classify the language that he or she has chosen to use. In order to find out what the biases of the author might be, we need to classify the "nature of the patterns of choice of content and language".[6]

This really demonstrates that the tools we apply in order to critically read a text include critical analysis and inference. And it is critical thinking that teaches us to critically analyse and infer.

KEY POINTS

Critical thinking, and critical reading and learning:

- Critical reading is a technique of:
  - i. Gathering ideas and information from a given text
  - ii. Evaluating these ideas and information
- To actively engage in what you are reading, you need to recognise the four preliminaries:
  - i. The subject matter
  - ii. The aim
  - iii. The relation between the subject and the aim
  - iv. The person to whom the text is addressed
- To be critical in thinking, we need to know:
  - i. What the text says
  - ii. What the text does
  - iii. What the text means

The third point is the most important as we need to interpret the text if we are to critically read it.

THINKING THROUGH EXERCISE 1

i. What is critical reading?

ii. What are the aims of critical reading?

5.3 Critically Thinking, Reading, and Writing

We now know what a critical thinker and what a critical reader must do. When we analyse some text as a critical thinker and as a critical reader, we look for certain specific qualities. This means, we need to demonstrate these same qualities in our writing as well. For instance, when we write, we need to be *clear, accurate and precise, write what is relevant, and cover the depth and breadth of the subject matter.* All this follows from the standards of critical thinking.

Following the classical Indian concept of *anuvandha catustaya* or the four preliminaries, we must:

i. Clearly state the subject matter
ii. State the aim of our writing
iii. State how a discussion of the subject matter might help to achieve this aim
iv. State who the writing is meant for

This is required because a clear statement of this would make the reader inclined to read what you have written and would also help the reader understand what the purpose of your writing is. We must also do the following:

i. Clearly state the claims you want to make
ii. Avoid ambiguity, vagueness, unwarranted generalisations and over-simplification of the issue
iii. Provide certain background information to the reader in order to make your claim clear and show its relevance:
   - ❑ Explain the academic and historical context of the discussion of the subject
   - ❑ Describe the audience the writing is addressed to
iv. Clearly and effectively argue each claim that you make
v. Show evidence for supporting your claim
vi. Use examples to instantiate your claim
vii. Explain all the concepts you use no matter how common those concepts may be
viii. Explain the theories you employ or assume in your writing. You must also support your choice of theories.
ix. Clearly explain the methodology adopted and state why this methodology is the right one for the subject matter at hand

As will be obvious from a cautious reading of what I have written, all these properties of critical writing follow from critical thinking and critical reading. What we are actually trying to do is convince the reader of what we write. There are a few questions we ought to ask in order to see for ourselves if our writing can indeed convince others:

i. "Is your position clearly stated? Is it in focus throughout the paper?
ii. Does your reasoning lead to a logical conclusion?
iii. Is your language understandable?

iv. Are your definitions clearly explained? Are they reasonable?
v. Is your writing clear and concise?
vi. Do you state and defend your assumptions?
vii. Is your position well informed?
viii. Are your sources identified? Are they credible?
ix. Are your generalizations reasonable?
x. Are your hypotheses and predictions sound?
xi. Have you covered well-known alternative views?
xii. Are you being fair and open-minded?
xiii. Will your paper convince your reader?"[7]

Usually, there are several things that we need to follow while writing. Here, we shall mention five:

i. Convention

In order to effectively write, we need to follow certain conventions. The conventions we have in mind are mostly linguistic in nature. When writing in English, for instance, we need to follow the conventions of Standard English. For example, students are often asked to use the literary present tense and the active voice instead of the passive voice. Students are also asked to avoid sentences that reflect personal points of view, unless asked to present their own views on the matter at hand. That is, they are typically asked to adopt an objective point of view. Students are also asked to avoid platitudes like, "This view is the one I like." When a student has to discuss a particular view, it is better to mention what follows from the view and not what impact the view has on the student's mind, and so the objective point of view is always preferred.

Students also have to be very cautious while quoting from other works. There are certain citation conventions when doing so. They are usually asked to select any one convention and follow it throughout. Whichever citation convention you select, you need to mention the following:

In case of a book:

- ❑ The name of the book, which should be written in italics
- ❑ The name of the author
- ❑ The name of the publisher
- ❑ The year of publication
- ❑ The place of publication
- ❑ The pages that are referred

In case of an article appearing in a journal:

- ❑ The name of the article, which should be written within quotes
- ❑ The name of the author

- ❑ The name of the journal
- ❑ The volume number or the date and year
- ❑ The pages on which the article occurs
- ❑ The pages being referred to

In case of an article from an anthology:

- ❑ The name of the article, which should be written within quotes
- ❑ The name of the author
- ❑ The name of the anthology in which the article is published, which should be written in italics
- ❑ The name of the editor/s of the anthology
- ❑ The name of the publisher
- ❑ The place of publication
- ❑ The year of publication
- ❑ The pages referred to

There may be other conventions that are specific to the discipline in which the study is being conducted. For example, there are conventions regarding lower case or upper case letters while symbolically representing sentences in formal logic.

ii. Sequencing

It is very important to sequence what we write. If we consider the ways in which a good teacher teaches, we will see why sequencing is so important. Sequencing is crucial in order to impart information and that is why teachers always sequence their lessons. This is how we might sequence what we say, what we teach or what we write:

- ❑ Introduction
  - ❑ Introducing the topic
  - ❑ Introducing the sub-topics
  - ❑ Explaining the sequence in which the sub-topics follow each other
- ❑ We must state the purpose of the study along with the introduction
- ❑ We should have what may be called an advance label of the section to follow
- ❑ We should recapitulate what we have said before when we are introducing a new topic
- ❑ There should be a statement of the position that you take in the study
- ❑ There should be a conclusion drawn, which might actually be the position you take
- ❑ There must be some indication of the questions that arise from the study and some directions for further research

iii. Signposting

Signposting and sequencing go hand in hand. Signposting in writing helps a writer link what has been written previously with what is written later on. There are certain linguistic ploys that we can use to link one part of our writing with another. Often, a simple *anaphora* helps in doing so. For example, we may use the word "this" to link two sentences, as in these sentences: "The rise in oil prices will lead to inflation. This will lead to a lot of hardship amongst common people." Here, the word "this" refers to inflation, which is mentioned in the first sentence. We often use sequence-indicating words like signposts. For instance, we write, "firstly … secondly …" or we might write "furthermore" or "as a result of". We have studied how when we present an argument, we often use indicator words to indicate the premises, which are signposts like "since", "because", "for" and indicator words for the conclusions, which are signposts like "hence", "therefore", "consequently" or "so".

The purpose of signposts is to give the reader some direction. Just as road signs direct travellers, signposts lead the reader in the direction the writer wants them to take. As authors, it is our duty to make our writing as clear as possible to the reader. This is why signposts, which are really like road signs, help the reader. A good writer should always pre-empt the questions that may arise in the mind of the reader while reading the text. It is to answer these questions that the writer must provide the critical reader directions pointing towards the author's aims and how these aims might be achieved. The critical thinker would also be keen on knowing the author's view on a particular matter for which the author should give clear indications. Signposts actually lead the reader to the answers of the queries she has while reading any text.

We have to remember that when we are presenting an argument, we should clearly state all its points and through this allow the argument to speak for itself. "A sound essay plan and a coherent structure will reveal the logic of your argument and the relationship of its parts."[8]

Signposts can be of two kinds:[9]

- "Major signposts that signal key aspects of the work, such as purpose, author's stance, main points, direction of the argument, conclusions
- Linking words and phrases that show connections between sentences and paragraphs."

Some examples of signposts are, "In this Chapter, I aim to discuss …", "The purpose of this study is …", "This paper argues that …", "This paper attempts at a critical evaluation of …" etc.

We have previously mentioned some examples of linking words and phrases, and here are the different kinds of linking words or phrases:

- "**Listing:**

  First(ly), second(ly), finally
- **Indicating addition or similarity:**

  Also, besides, in addition, furthermore, as well, similarly
- **Indicating contrast:**

  However, nevertheless, on the other hand

- **Giving a reason:**
  For this reason, because, because of, due to
- **Indicating result:**
  Therefore, thus, as a result, consequently, yet
- **Reformulating an idea:**
  In other words, to put it simply, that is
- **Exemplifying:**
  For example, for instance, to exemplify"[10]

iv. Structuring

As is already clear, writing should always have a clear structure. Structured writing is the result of a writing plan, that is, a clear and well-knit logical sequence of all parts that constitute the text. How we sequence our sections or how the logic runs will vary from case to case and will depend on many factors such as:

- "Logical progression
- Increasing significance
- Equal significance
- Chronological order
- Narrative sequence
- Category groupings"[11]

v. A sense of the audience

As we have discussed, the critical writer must always be aware of the audience that she is addressing through her writing. This is why a writer must develop a sense of audience. This is an issue that has been frequently discussed in great depth in a large amount of literature and we will therefore not delve into it in detail. However, we will simply say that in developing a sense of audience, we need to be aware of the context of the discussion and also have some idea of the background knowledge that the readers might be expected to have. A critical writer should keep these two things in mind to produce writing that is effective for her readers.

KEY POINTS

Critically thinking, reading and writing

- Critical reading and critical thinking facilitates critical writing
- To be a critical writer, we should:
  - i. Write clearly
  - ii. Aviod ambiguity, vagueness, unwarranted generalisations and oversimplification of issues

iii. Provide background information
iv. Effectively argue the claim
v. Provide evidence for the claims made
vi. Use examples to explain concepts and theories
vii. Describe the methodology adopted

- A critically written text should:
  i. Follow convention
  ii. Be properly sequenced
  iii. Use proper signposting techniques
  iv. Be well structured
  v. Respect its audience

THINKING THROUGH EXERCISE 2

i. What is critical writing?
ii. How can we become critical writers?

5.4 Concluding Remarks

We have now come to the end of this book. In this book, we have discussed quite a few topics, though briefly. In the first chapter, we discussed who a critical thinker is and what can make a critical thinker a good one. We have also discussed the standards of critical thinking as well as its benefits and barriers. In the second chapter, we discussed what an argument is and how we can recognise an argument. Here, we discussed premises, hidden premises, conclusions and intermediate conclusions, truth content and logical content, validity, deductive arguments, inductive arguments and strength. Then, in the third chapter, we discussed inferences and fallacies, how certain linguistic phenomena contribute to fallacious arguments, fallacies and specifically relevance. In chapter four, we discussed information and its evaluation as well as the various sources of information. We discussed the basic human limitations with regard to reason and its social influences. Finally, in this chapter, we discussed how critical thinking enhances critical reading and how critical thinking and critical reading promotes critical writing.

Critical thinking is not only for the chosen few, not only for the academically inclined, not only for those who receive a formal higher education but is for any reasonable human being, any rational agent and any responsible citizen of a country. I am certain that while reading this book, many of my readers may have felt like they are already aware of a lot of what we have said about critical thinking. Perhaps many also felt they do not need this training in critical thinking because they already are critical thinkers. Just as we need to study grammar though we are perfectly fluent and correct in our native language, we need to study ways of critical reasoning just in order to re-instil an almost natural ability that human beings are blessed with—the ability to think critically.

5.5 More Exercises

Answer the following questions:

1. Who is a critical reader?
2. What are the four preliminaries? Why are they relevant for critical reading and critical writing?
3. What are the things that we need to check when we evaluate a written work as a reader?
4. What are the nine things that a critical reader has to do?
5. What are the conventions of critical writing?
6. How do we sequence our writing?
7. What are signposts?
8. How do we structure our writing?
9. What do we mean by sense of audience?

NOTES AND REFERENCES

1. Marcus Tullius Cicero, Roman author, orator and politician (106 BC–43 BC).

2. Dan Kurland, http://www.criticalreading.com/critical_reading_thinking.htm, accessed on 2 May 2009.

3. Barbara Feldman, http://www.surfnetkids.com/safety/the_ten_cs_of_information_evaluation-29273.htm, accessed on 2 May 2009.

4. Dan Kurland, http://www.criticalreading.com/critical_reading.htm, accessed on 2 May 2009.

5. http://www.surfnetkids.com/safety/the_ten_cs_of_information_evaluation-29273.htm, accessed on 4 May 2009.

6. Dan Kurland, http://www.criticalreading.com/critical_reading.htm, accessed on 4 May 2009.

7. http://classes.aces.uiuc.edu/ACES100/Mind/CritWtg.html, accessed on 4 May 2009.

8. http://www.mantex.co.uk/ou/a319/a319-13.htm, accessed on 4 May 2009.

9. http://www.ncl.ac.uk/students/wdc/learning/language/signposting.htm, accessed on 4 May 2009.

10. Ibid., accessed on 6 May 2009.

11. http://www.mantex.co.uk/ou/a319/a319-13.htm.

INDEX